LETTER.

FELLOW-CITIZENS OF THE UNITED STATES:

IT may seem strange and presumptuous that an obscure man, known even by name to but very few in the land, should write you a public letter on a theme so important as this of Slavery. You may call it foolish and rash. Say that if you will; perhaps you are right. I have no name, no office, no rank amongst men, which entitle my thoughts to your consideration. I am but one of the undistinguished millions, who live unnoticed, and die remembered only by their family and friends; humble and obscure. If any of the famous men accustomed to sway the opinions of the political parties and the theological sects, had suitably treated this matter, showing you the facts and giving manly counsel, I should not have presumed to open my mouth. It is their silence which prompts me to speak. I am no aspirant for office or for fame; have nothing to gain by your favor; fear nothing from your frown. In writing this Letter I obey no idle caprice, but speak from a sense of Duty, in

1

submission to the voice of Conscience. I love my Country, and my Kind; it is Patriotism and Humanity which bid me speak. I ask you to read and consider, not to read without your prejudices, but with them, with them all; then to consider, to decide, to act, as you may or must. I address myself to no party, to no sect, but speak to you, as Americans and as Men, addressing my thoughts to all the Citizens of the Slave States and the Free.

I am to speak of a great evil, long established, wide spread, deeply rooted in the laws, the usages and the ideas of the people. It affects directly the welfare of three millions of men, one sixth part of the nation: they are Slaves. It affects directly half the States: they are Slave-holders. It has a powerful influence on the other half, though more subtle and unseen. It affects the industry, laws, morals, and entire prosperity of the whole nation to a degree exceeding the belief of men not familiar with its history and its facts. The evil increases with a rapid growth; with advancing flood it gains new territory, swells with larger volume; its deadly spray and miasma gradually invade all our institutions. The whole nation is now legally pledged to its support; the public legislation for the last sixty years has made Slavery a federal institution. Your revenue boats and your navy are bound to support it; your army acts for its defence. You have fought wars, spending money and shedding blood, to gain new soil wherein to plant the tree of Slavery. You have established it in your districts and your territories.. You have recently annexed to your realm a new territory as large as the Kingdom of France, and extended Slavery over that soil whence a semi-barbarous people had expelled it with ignominy. You are now fighting a war in behalf of Slavery, a war carried on at great cost of money and of men. The national capital is a great slave market; in her shambles your Brothers are daily offered for sale. Your flag floats over the most wicked commerce on earth — the traffic in men and women. Citizens of the United States breed youths and maidens for sale in the market, as the grazier oxen and swine.

The Bey of Tunis has abolished Slavery as a disgrace to Africa and the Mahometan religion. Your Constitution of the United States supports this institution, and binds it upon the free States; the South fondly clings to it; the free men of the North bend suppliant necks to this yoke. With a few exceptions, your Representatives and Senators in Congress give it their countenance and their vote; their hand and their heart. Your great and famous men are pledged to this, or their silence practically purchased. Seven Presidents of your Christian Democracy have been holders of slaves; three only free from that taint. You will soon be called on to elect another Slave-holder to sit in the presi-

dential chair, and rule over a republic containing twenty millions of men.

In all the Union there is no legal asylum for the
fugitive slave; no soil emancipates his hurrying
feet. The States which allow no Slavery within
their limits legally defend the Slave-holder: catch
and retain the man fleeing for his manhood and his
life.

I cannot call upon the political leaders of the
nation. You know what they look for, and how
they would treat a letter exposing a national evil,
and talking of Truth and Justice. I do not address
you as members of the political parties; they have
their great or petty matters to deal with, differing
in regard to free trade or protection, but are
united in one policy as it respects Slavery. Demagogues of both parties will play their little game,
and on your shoulders ride into fame, and ease,
and wealth, and power, and noise. The sects also
have their special work, and need not be addressed
on the subject of Slavery — of human wrong.

I speak to the People, not as Sectarians, Pro-
testant or Catholic — not as Democrats or Whigs,
but as Americans and as Men. I solemnly believe
if you all knew the facts of American Slavery and
its effects, as I know them, that you would end the
evil before a twelvemonth had passed by. I take
it for granted that you love Justice and Truth. I
write to you, having confidence in your integrity

and love of men, having confidence also in the democratic ideas on which a government should rest.

In what I write you will doubtless find mistakes — errors of fact or of reasoning. I do not ask to be screened from censure even for what no diligence could wholly escape, only that you will not reject nor refuse to consider the truth of fact and of reasoning which is presented to you. A few mistakes in figures or in reasoning will not affect the general argument of this Letter. Read with what prejudice you may, but decide and act according to Reason and Conscience.

I.

I WILL first call your attention to the Statistics and History of Slavery. In 1790 there were but 697,897 Slaves in the Union; in 1840, 2,487,355. At the present day their number probably is not far from 3,000,000. In 1790, Mr. Gerry estimated their value at $10,000,000; in 1840 Mr. Clay fixed it at $1,200,000,000. They are owned by a population of perhaps about 300,000 persons, and represented by about 100,000 voters.

At the time of the Declaration of Independence Slavery existed in all the States; it gradually receded from the North. In the religious Colonies of New England it was always unpopular and odious. It was there seen and felt to be utterly inconsistent with the ideas and spirit of their institutions, their Churches and their State itself. After the Revolution therefore it speedily disappeared — here perishing by default, there abolished by statute. Thus it successively disappeared from Rhode Island, Massachusetts, New Hampshire,

New York, Pennsylvania, and New Jersey. By the celebrated Ordinance of 1787, involuntary servitude, except as a punishment after legal conviction of crime, was forever prohibited in the North West Territory. Thus the new States, formed in the Western parallels, were, by the action of the federal government, at once cut off from that institution. Besides, they were mainly settled by men from the Eastern States, who had neither habits nor principles which favored Slavery. Thus Ohio, Indiana, Illinois, Michigan, Wisconsin, and Iowa, have been without any legal slaves from the beginning.

In the South the character of the people was different; their manners, their social and political ideas were unlike those of the North. The Southern States were mainly colonies of adventurers, rather than establishments of men who for conscience' sake fled to the wilderness. Less pains were taken with the education — intellectual, moral, and religious — of the people. Religion never held so prominent a place in the consciousness of the mass as in the sterner and more austere colonies of the North. In the Southern States — New Jersey, Delaware, Maryland, Virginia, the Carolinas, and Georgia, — Slavery easily found a footing at an early day. It was not at all repulsive to the ideas, the institutions and habits of Georgia and South Carolina. The other Southern States protested against it ; — they never.

Consequences follow causes; it is not easy to avoid the results of a first principle. The Northern States, in all their constitutions and social structure, consistently and continually tend to Democracy — the government of all, for all, and by all; — to equality before the State and its Laws; to moral and political ideas of universal application. In the meantime the Southern States, in their constitutions and social structure, as consistently tend to Oligarchy — the government over all, by a few, and for the sake of that few; — to privilege, favoritism, and class-legislation; to conventional limitations; to the rule of force, and inequality before the law. In such a state of things when Slavery comes, it is welcome. In 1787, South Carolina and Geórgia refused to accept the federal Constitution unless the right of importing Slaves was guaranteed to them for twenty years. The new States formed in the Southern parallels — Kentucky, Tennessee, Alabama, Mississippi — retaining the ideas and habits of their parents, kept also the institution of Slavery.

At the time of forming the Federal Constitution some of the southern statesmen were hostile to Slavery, and would gladly have got rid of it. Economical considerations prevailed in part, but political and moral objections to it extended yet more widely. The Ordinance of 1787, the work mainly of the same man who drafted the Declaration of

Independence, passed with little opposition. The proviso for surrendering fugitive slaves came from a northern hand. Subsequently opposition to Slavery, in the north and the south, became less. The culture of cotton, the wars in Europe creating a demand for the productions of American agriculture, had rendered slave labor more valuable. The day of our own oppression was more distant and forgotten. So in 1802, when Congress purchased from Georgia the western part of her territory, it was easy for the South to extend Slavery over that virgin soil. In 1803, Louisiana was purchased from France; then, or in 1804, when it was organized into two territories, it would have been easy to apply the Ordinance of 1787, and prevent Slavery from extending beyond the original thirteen States. But though some provisions restricting Slavery were made, the ideas of that Ordinance were forgotten. Since that time five new States have been formed out of territory acquired since the revolution : — Louisiana, Missouri, Arkansas, Florida, Texas, all Slave States, — the last two with constitutions aiming to make Slavery perpetual. The last of these was added to the Union on the 22d of December, 1845, two hundred and twenty-five years after the day when the Forefathers first set foot on Plymouth Rock; while the sons of the Pilgrims were eating and drinking and making merry, the deed of Annexation was completed, and

2

Slavery extended over nearly 400,000 square miles of new territory, whence the semi-barbarous Mexicans had driven it out.

Slavery might easily have been abolished at the time of the Declaration of Independence. Indeed in 1774 the Continental Congress, in their celebrated " non-importation Agreement," resolved never to import or purchase any slaves after the last of December in that year. In 1775, they declare in a " Report " that it is not possible " for men who exercise their reason to believe that the divine Author of our existence intended a part of the human race to hold an absolute property in and unbounded power over others." Indeed the Declaration itself is a denial of the national right to allow the existence of Slavery : " We hold these truths to be self-evident, that all men are created equal ; that they are endowed by their Creator with certain unalienable rights, that among these are [the right to] life, liberty, and the pursuit of happiness ; — that to secure these rights governments are instituted among men deriving their just powers from the consent of the governed."

But the original draft of this paper contained a condemnation yet more explicit : " He [the king of England] has waged cruel war against human nature itself ; violating its most sacred rights of life and iberty in the persons of a distant people who never offended him; captivating and carrying them into slavery....Determined to keep open a market where men should be bought and sold, he has prostituted his negative for suppressing every legislative attempt to prohibit or restrain this execrable commerce." This clause, says its author himself, "was struck out in compliance to South Carolina and Georgia, who had never attempted to restrain the importation of slaves, and who, on the contrary, still wished to continue it. Our northern brethren also, I believe, felt a little tender under these censures; for though their people have very few slaves themselves, yet they had been pretty considerable carriers of them to others.".

These were not the sentiments of a single enthusiastic young Republican. Dr. Rush, in the Continental Congress, wished "the Colonies to discourage Slavery and encourage the increase of the free inhabitants." Another member of the American congress declared, in 1779, " Men are by nature free;" "the right to be free can never be alienated." In 1776, Dr. Hopkins, the head of the New England divines, declared that " Slavery is, in every instance, wrong, unrighteous and oppressive; a very great and crying sin."

In the articles of Confederation, adopted in 1778, no provision is made for the support of Slavery; none for the delivery of fugitives. Slavery is not

once referred to in that document. The General
Government had nothing to do with it. " If any
slave elopes to those states where slaves are free,"
said Mr. Madison in 1787, " he becomes emancipated by their laws."

In the Convention of 1787, which drafted the present Constitution of the United States, this matter
of Slavery was abundantly discussed ; it was the
great obstacle in the way of forming the Union, as
now of keeping it. But for the efforts of South
Carolina, it is probable Slavery would have been
abolished by the Constitution. The South claimed
the right of sending Representatives to Congress on
account of their Slaves. Mr. Patterson, of New
Jersey, contended that as the slaves had no representative or vote at home, their masters could not
claim additional votes in Congress on account of the
slaves. Nearly all the speakers in that Convention,
except the members from South Carolina and Georgia, referred to the slave-trade with horror. Mr.
Gerry, of Massachusetts, declared in the Convention, that it was " as humiliating to enter into com-
pact with the slaves of the Southern States, as with
the horses and mules of the North." It was contended, that if slaves were men, then they should be
taxed as men, and have their vote as men ; if mere
property, they should not entitle their owners to a
vote, more than other property. It might be proper
to tax slaves, " because it had a tendency to dis-

courage Slavery, but to take them into account in giving representatives tended to encourage the slave trade, and to make it the interest of the States to continue that infamous traffic." It was said, that " we had just assumed a place among independent nations, in consequence of our opposition to the attempts of Great Britain to enslave us; that this opposition was grounded upon the preservation of those rights to which God and Nature had entitled us, not in particular, but in common with all the rest of mankind. That we had appealed to the Supreme Being for his assistance, as the God of heaven, who could not but approve our efforts to preserve the rights which he had imparted to his creatures; that now, when we had scarcely risen from our knees from supplicating his aid and protection in forming our government over a free people, — a government formed pretendedly on the principles of liberty, and for its preservation, — in that government to have a provision, not only putting it out of its power to restrain or prevent the slave trade, even encouraging that most infamous traffic, and giving States power and influence in the Union in proportion as they cruelly and wantonly sport with the rights of their fellow creatures, — ought to be considered as a solemn mockery of, and insult to, that God, whose protection we had then implored, and could not fail to hold us up in detesta-

2*

tion, and render us contemptible to every true
friend of liberty in the world."

Luther Martin, the attorney-general of Maryland,
thought it "inconsistent with the principles of the
Revolution, and dishonorable to the American
character," to have the importation of slaves allowed by the Constitution.

The Northern States, and some of the Southern,
wished to abolish the slave trade at once. Mr.
Pinckney, of South Carolina, thought that State
"would never accede to the Constitution, if it
prohibits the slave trade ;" she "would not stop
her importation of slaves in any short time." Said
Mr. Rutledge, of South Carolina, "the people of
the Carolinas and Georgia, will never be such fools
as to give up so important an interest." "Religion
and humanity have nothing to do with this question.
Interest alone is the governing principle with nations." In apportioning taxes, he thought three
slaves ought to be counted as but one free man ;
while in apportioning representatives, his colleagues,
— Messrs. Butler and Pinckney, — declared, "the
Blacks ought to stand on an equality with the
Whites." Mr. Pinckney would "make Blacks
equal to Whites in the ratio of representation ;" he
went further, — he would have "some security
against an emancipation of slaves ;" and, says Mr.
Madison, "seemed to wish some provision should
be included [in the Constitution] in favor of pro-

perty in slaves." "South Carolina and Georgia" said Mr. Pinckney, "cannot do without slaves;" "The importation of slaves would be for the interest of the whole Union; the more slaves, the more produce to employ the carrying trade, the more consumption also."

On the other hand, Mr. Bedford of Delaware, thought "South Carolina was puffed up with her wealth and her negroes." Mr. Madison, cool and far-sighted, always referring to first principles, was unwilling to allow the importation of slaves till 1808 :— " So long a term will be more dishonorable to the American character than to say nothing about it in the constitution."

Mr. Williamson of North Carolina, in 1783, thought "slaves an incumbrance to society," and was " both in opinion and practice against Slavery." Col. Mann, of Virginia, in the Convention, called the slave trade an " infernal traffic," and said that " Slavery discourages arts and manufactures ; the poor despise labor when performed by slaves." " They produce the most pernicious effect on manners. Every master of slaves is born a petty tyrant. They bring the judgment of Heaven on a country." Mr. Dickinson, of Delaware, thought it " inadmissible on every principle of honor and safety that the importation of slaves should be authorized." Gôuverneur Morris, of Pennsylvania " never would concur in upholding domestic

Slavery." It was a "nefarious institution;" "the curse of Heaven was on the States where it prevailed!" Are the slaves men? "then make them citizens, and let them vote. Are they property? Why then is no other property included [in the ratio of representation]? The houses in this city [Philadelphia] are worth more than all the wretched slaves who cover the rice-swamps of South Carolina." Mr. Gerry declared we "ought to be careful not to give any sanction to it."

All the North was at first opposed to Slavery and the slave trade. Both parties seemed obstinate; the question of "Taxes on exports" and of "Navigation laws" remained to be decided. Gouverneur Morris recommended that the whole subject of Slavery might be referred to a committee "including the clauses relating to the taxes on exports, and to the navigation laws. These things may form a bargain among the Northern and Southern States." Says Luther Martin, "I found the Eastern States, notwithstanding their aversion to Slavery, were very willing to indulge the Southern States, at least with a temporary liberty to prosecute the slave trade, provided the Southern States would in their turn gratify them by laying no restriction on navigation acts." The North began to understand if the contemplated navigation laws should be enacted, that as Mr. Grayson afterwards said, " all the produce of the Southern States will be carried by the Northern States on their own terms, which must be high." Mr. Clymer, of Pennsylvania, declared, " The Western and Middle States will be ruined, if not enabled to defend themselves against foreign regulations ; " will be ruined if they do not have some navigation laws giving Americans an advantage over foreign vessels. Mr. Gorham, of Massachusetts, said " The Eastern States had no motives to union but a commercial one." The proffered compromise would favor their commercial interests. It was for the commercial interest of the South said Mr. Pinckney, to have no restrictions upon commerce, but " considering the loss brought on the Eastern States by the Revolution, and their liberal conduct towards the views of South Carolina, [in consenting to allow Slavery and the importation of slaves,] he thought that no fetters should be imposed on the power of making commercial regulations, and his constituents would be reconciled to the liberality." So the North took the boon, and winked at the " infernal traffic." When the question was put, there were in favor of the importation of slaves, Georgia, the two Carolinas and Maryland, with New Hampshire, Massachusetts and Connecticut. Opposed to it were Pennsylvania, New Jersey, Delaware and Virginia ! Subsequently Mr. Ames, in the Massachusetts Convention for the adoption of the Constitution, said the Northern States " have great advantages by it in respect of navigation;" in the Virginia Convention Patrick Henry said, "Tobacco will always make our peace with them," for at that time Cotton was imported from India, not having become a staple of the South.   When the article which binds the free States to deliver up the fugitive slaves, came to be voted on, it was a new feature in American legislation; not hinted at in the "articles of confederation;" hostile to the well known principles of the common law of England — which always favors liberty — and the usages and principles of modern civilized nations.   Yet new as it was and hostile, it seems not a word was said against it in the Convention.   It "was agreed to, *nem. con.*"   Yet "The Northern delegates," says Mr. Madison, "owing to their particular scruples on the subject of Slavery, did not choose the word slave to be mentioned."   In the conventions of the several States it seems no remonstrance was made to this article.

Luther Martin returning home, said to the House of Delegates in Maryland, "At this time we do not generally hold this commerce in so great abhorrence as we have done; when our liberties were at .stake, we warmly felt for the common rights of men; the danger being thought to be past, we are daily growing more insensible to their rights."

When the several States came to adopt the Constitution, some hesitancy was shown at tolerating the slave trade or even Slavery itself. In the Massachusetts convention, Mr. Neal would not "favor the making merchandise of the bodies of men." Gen. Thompson exclaimed, " shall it be said, that after we have established our own independence and freedom we make slaves of others ?" Washington has immortalized himself, " but he holds those in slavery who have as good a right to be free as he has." All parties deprecated the slave trade in most pointed terms. " Slavery was generally detested." It was thought that the new States could not claim the sad privilege of their parents, that the South itself would soon hate and abolish it. " Slavery is not smitten by an apoplexy," said Mr. Dawes, " yet it has received a mortal wound and will die of consumption." This reflection, with the " Tobacco " and " Navigation laws " turned the scale. Patrick Henry was no son of New England, but knew well on what hinges her political morality might turn, by what means and which way.

In the New York Convention, Mr. Smith could "not see any rule by which slaves were to be included in the ratio of representation, the very operation of it was to give certain privileges to men who were so wicked as to keep slaves;" to which Mr. Hamilton replied, that " without this indulgence no union could possibly have been formed. But . . considering those peculiar advantages which we derived from them, [the Southern

States,] it is entirely just that they should be grati-
fied. The Southern States possess certain staples,
tobacco, rice, indigo, &c. which must be capital objects in treaties of commerce with foreign nations;
and the advantage . . . will be felt in all the States."

In the Pennsylvania Convention, Mr. Wilson considered that the constitution laid the foundation for
abolishing Slavery out of this country," though the
period was more distant than he could wish. Yet
" the New States . . . will be under the control of Congress in this particular, and slavery will never be
introduced amongst them ;" " yet the lapse of a
few years, and congress will have power to exter-
minate slavery from within our borders."

In the Virginia convention Gov. Randolph regarded the slave trade as " infamous" and " detestable."
Slavery was one of our vulnerable points. " Are
we not weakened by the population of those whom
we hold in slavery"? he asked. Col. Mason thought
the trade " diabolical in itself and disgraceful to
mankind." He would not admit the Southern
States [Georgia and the Carolinas] into the Union
unless they agreed to the discontinuance of this
disgraceful trade." Mr. Tyler thought " nothing
could justify it." Patrick Henry, who contended
for Slavery, confessed " Slavery is detested, — we
feel its fatal effects, — we deplore it with all the
pity of humanity." " It would rejoice my very
soul that every one of my fellow-beings was eman-

cipated." Said **Mr. Johnson**, "Slavery has been the foundation of that impiety and dissipation which have been so much disseminated among our countrymen. If it were **totally** abolished it would do much good."

In the North Carolina Convention it was found necessary to apologize for the pro-slavery character of the Constitution. **Mr.** Iredell in defence said, the matter of Slavery "was regulated with great difficulty and by a spirit of concession which it would not be prudent to disturb for a good many years." "It is probable that all the members reprobated this inhuman traffic [in slaves], but those of South Carolina and Georgia would not consent to an immediate prohibition of it." "Were it practicable to put an end to the importation of slaves immediately, it would give him the greatest pleasure." "When the entire abolition of Slavery takes place it will be an event which must be pleasing to every generous mind and every friend of human nature." **Mr. McDowall** looked upon the slave trade "as a very objectionable part of the system." **Mr. Goudy** did not wish "to be represented with negroes."

In the South Carolina Convention Gen. Pinckney admitted that the Carolinas and Georgia were so weak that they "could not form a union strong enough for the purpose of effectually protecting each other;" it was their policy therefore "to

3

form a close union with the Eastern States who are
strong;" the Eastern States had been the greatest
sufferers in the Revolution, they had " lost every-
thing but their country and their freedom ;" " we,"
the Carolinas and Georgia, " should let them, in
some measure, partake of our prosperity." But
the union could come only from a compromise ;
" we have secured an unlimited importation of
negroes for twenty years." " We have obtained
a right to recover our slaves in whatever part of
America they shall take refuge, which is a right we
had not before." " We have made the best terms
for the security of this species of property it was in
our power to make ; we would have made better if
we could, but on the whole I do not think them
bad." No one in South Carolina, it seems, thought
Slavery an Evil.

Thus the Constitution was assented to as " the result of accommodation," though containing clauses
confessedly " founded on unjust principles." The
North had been false to its avowed convictions, and
in return " higher tonnage duties were imposed on
foreign than on American bottoms," and goods imported in American vessels " paid ten per cent. less
duty than the same goods brought in those owned
by foreigners." The " Navigation laws " and the
" Tobacco " wrought after their kind ; South Carolina and Georgia had their way. The North, said

Gouverneur Morris, in the national Convention, for the " sacrifice of every principle of right, of every impulse of humanity," had this compensation, " to bind themselves to march their militia for the defence of the Southern States, for their defence against those very slaves of whom they complain. They must supply vessels and seamen in case of foreign attack. The legislature will have indefinite power to tax them by excises and duties on imports."

Still, with many there lingered a vague belief that Slavery would soon perish. In the first Congress Mr. Jackson, of Georgia, admitted that " it was an evil habit." Mr. Gerry and Mr. Madison both thought that Congress had " the right to regulate this business," and " if they see proper, to make a proposal to purchase all the slaves." But the most obvious time for ending the institution had passed by ; the feeling of hostility to it grew weaker and weaker as the nation became united, powerful and rich ; its " mortal wound " was fast getting healed.

II.

I WILL next consider the General Condition and
Treatment of the Slaves themselves. The slave
is not, theoretically, considered as a Person; he is
only a Thing, as much so as an axe or a spade;
accordingly he is wholly subject to his master, and
has no Rights — which are an attribute of Persons
only, not of Things. All that he enjoys therefore
is but a Privilege. He may be damaged but not
wronged. However ill treated he cannot of himself, in his own name and right, bring a formal
action in any court; no more than an axe or a
spade, though his master may bring an action for
damages. The slave cannot appear as a witness
when a freeman is on trial. His master can beat,
maim, mutilate, or mangle him, and the slave has,
theoretically, no complete and legal redress, practically, no redress at all. The master may force
him to marry or forbid his marriage; can sell him
away from wife and children. He can force the
lover to beat his beloved; the husband his wife,
the child his parent. " A slave is one who is in

the power of his master, to whom he belongs. The
master may sell him, dispose of his person, his industry and his labor; he can do nothing, possess
nothing, nor acquire anything but what must be-
long to his master." No contract between master
and slave, however solemnly made and attested,
is binding on the master. Is the freeborn child of
the free man likewise theoretically subject to his
father ? — natural and instinctive affection prevent
the abuse of that power. The connection between
father and child is one of guardianship and recipro-
cal love, a mutual gain ; that of master and slave
is founded only on the interest of the owner; the
gain is only on the master's side.

The relation of master and slave begins in violence; it must be sustained by violence — the
systematic violence of general laws, or the irregular violence of individual caprice. There is no other
mode of conquering and subjugating a man. Re-
garding the slave as a thing, "an instrument of
husbandry," the master gives him the least, and
takes the most that is possible. He takes all the
result of the slave's toil, leaving only enough to keep
him in a profitable working condition. His work
is the most he can be made to do ; his food, clothing, shelter, amusement, the least he can do with.
" A southern Planter," in his " Notes on Political
Economy as applicable to the United States," says

3*

to his fellow slave-holders: " You own this labor, can regulate it, work it many or few hours in the day, accelerate it, stimulate it, control it, avoid turn-outs and combinations, and pay no wages. You can dress it plainly, feed it coarsely and cheap, lodge it, on simple forms, as the plantations do, house it in cabins costing little." " The slaves live without beds or houses worth so calling, or family cares, or luxuries, or parade or show; have no relaxations, or whims, or frolics or dissipations; instead of sun to sun, in their hours are worked from daylight till nine o'clock at night. Where the free man or laborer would require a hundred dollars a year for food and clothing alone, the slave can be supported for twenty dollars a year, and often is." " Let us bestow upon them the worst, the most unhealthy and degrading sort of duties and labor." Said Mr. Jefferson, " the whole commerce between master and slave is a perpetual exercise of the most boisterous passions, the most unremitting despotism on the one part, and degrading submission on the other."

The Idea of Slavery is to use a man as a thing, against his nature and in opposition to his interests. The consequences of such a principle it is impossible to escape; the results of this idea meet us at every step. Man is certainly not cruel by nature; even in the barbarous state. In our present civiliza-

tion man is far from being brutal. There are many
kind and considerate slave-holders whose aim is to
make their slaves as comfortable and happy as it is
possible while they are slaves ; men who feel and
know that Slavery is wrong, and would gladly be
rid of it ; who are not consistent with the idea of
Slavery. Let us suppose, in this argument, there are
ten thousand such who are heads of families in the
United States, and ninety thousand of a different
stamp, men who have at least the average of human selfishness.

Now under the mildest and most humane of
masters, Slavery commonly brings intensity of suffering. The slave feels that he is a Man, a Person,
his own Person, born with all a man's unalienable
rights ; born with the right to life, to liberty, and
the pursuit of happiness. He sees himself cut off
from these rights, and that too amid the wealth,
the refinement, and culture of this country and
this age. He feels his degradation, born a man
to be treated as a thing, bought and sold, beaten
as a beast. Here and there is one with a feeble
nature, with affections disproportionately strong,
attached to an owner who never claimed all the
legal authority of master, and this man may not
desire his freedom. Some hear of the actual
sufferings of the free blacks, or exaggerated re-
ports thereof, and fear that by becoming free in
America they might exchange a well-known evil

for a greater or a worse. Others have become so
debased by their condition that the man is mainly
silenced in their consciousness, the animal alone
surviving, contented if well fed and not over-
worked, and they do not wish to be free. Suppose
that these three classes, the feeble-minded, the timid,
and the men overwhelmed and crushed by their
condition, are as numerous as the humane portion
of the masters, are one-tenth of the whole, or
300,000. The rest are conscious of the qualities of a
man. They desire their freedom, and are kept in
Slavery only by external force — the systematic force
of public law, the irregular force of private will.
The number of this class will be about 2,700,000,
a greater number than the whole population of the
colonies in 1776.

The condition of the majority of the slaves is indeed terrible. They have no Rights, and are to be
treated not as Men, but only as Things; this first
principle involves continual violence and oppression,
with all the subordinate particulars of their condition, which shall now be touched on as briefly as
possible. A famous man said in public, that his
" slaves were sleek and fat ; " the best thing he
could say in defence of his keeping men in bondage. But even this is not always true. Take the
mass of slaves together, and an abundance of testimony compels the conviction, that they are misera-

bly clad, and suffer bitterly from hunger. So far as
food, clothing and shelter are concerned, the physi-
cal condition of the mass of field-slaves, is far worse
than that of condemned criminals, in the worst
prison of the United States. House-slaves and me-
chanics in large towns fare better ; they are under
the eye of the public. Farm-slaves feel most the
poignant smart. The plantations are large, the
dwellings distant, the ear of the public hears not the
oppressor's violence. " The horse fattens on his
master's eye," says the proverb; but the farm-
slaves are committed mainly to overseers, the Swiss
of Slavery, whom Mr. Wirt calls " the most abject,
degraded and unprincipled race."

Let us pass over the matter of food, clothing, shelter and toil, to consider other features of their condition. They are treated with great cruelty ; often
branded with a red hot iron on the breast, or the
shoulder, the arm, the forehead or the cheek,
though the Roman law forbid it fifteen centuries
ago. They are disfigured and mutilated, now by
the madness of anger, then by the jealous malice of
revenge, their backs and sides scored with the lash,
or bruised with the " paddle," bear marks of the
violence needful to subdue manhood still smoul-
dering in the ashes of the negro slave. Drive Nature out with whips and brands — she will come
back. These abuses can be proved from descrip-
tions of run-aways in the newspapers of the South.

The slaveholder's temptation to cruelty is too much for common men. His power is irresponsible. 'T is easy to find a stick if you would beat a dog. The lash is always at hand ; if a slave disobeys, — the whip ; if he is idle, — the whip ; does he murmur, — the whip ; is he sullen and silent, — the whip ; is the female coy and reluctant, — the whip. Chains and dungeons also are at hand. The Slave is a Thing ; judge and jury no friends to him. The condition of the Weak is bad enough everywhere, in Old England, and in New England. But when the Strong owns the very Bodies of the Weak, making and executing the laws as he will — it is not hard to see to what excess their wrongs will amount, wrongs which cannot be told.

It is often said that the evils of Slavery are exaggerated. This is said by the masters. But the story of the victim when told by his oppressor — it is well known what that is. The few slaves who can tell the story of their wrongs, show that Slavery cannot easily be represented as worse than it is. Imagination halts behind the fact. The lives of Moses Roper, of Lunsford Lane, of Moses Grundy, Frederic Douglas, and W. W. Brown, are before the public, and prove what could easily be learned from the advertisements of Southern newspapers, conjectured from the laws of the Southern States, or foretold outright from a knowledge of human nature itself : — that the sufferings of three millions of slaves form a mass of misery which the imagination can never realize, till the eye is familiar with its terrible details. Governor Giles, of Virginia, calls Slavery " a punishment of the highest order." And Mr. Preston says, " Happiness is incompatible with Slavery."

In the most important of all relations, that of man and wife, neither law nor custom gives protection to the slave. Their connection may at any moment be dissolved by the master's command, the parties be torn asunder, separated forever, husband and wife, child and mother ; the infant may be taken from its mother's breast, and sold away out of her sight and power. The wife torn from her husband's arms, forced to the lust of another, for the slave is no Person but a Thing. For the chastity of the female there is no defence ; no more than for the chastity of sheep and swine. Many are ravished in tender years. So is the last insult, and outrage the most debasing, added to this race of Americans. By the laws of Louisiana, all children born of slaves are reckoned as " natural and illegitimate." Marriage is " prostitution " ; sacred and permanent neither in the eyes of the churches nor the law. The female slave is wholly in her master's power. Mulattoes are more valuable than blacks. So in the Slave States Lust now leagues with Cupidity, and now acts with singleness of aim.

The South is full of mulattoes; its "best blood flows
in the veins of the slaves" — masters owning children white as themselves.   Girls, the children of
mulattoes, are sold at great price, as food for private licentiousness, or public furniture in houses of
ill-fame.   Under the worst of the Roman emperors
this outrage was forbidden, and the Prefect of the
city gave such slaves their freedom.   But republican parents not rarely sell their own children for
that abuse.

   After the formal and legal abolition of the African
slave trade, it became more profitable to breed
slaves for sale in the Northern Slave-holding States.
Their labor was of comparatively little value to the
declining agriculture of Delaware, Maryland, Virginia, and North Carolina.   From Planting they
have become, to a great degree, Slave-breeding
States.   The reputed sons of the " Cavaliers " have
found a new calling, and the " chivalry of the Old
Dominion" betakes itself, not to manufactures,
commerce, or agriculture, — but to the breeding of
slaves for the Southern market.   Kentucky and
Tennessee have embarked largely in the same ad-
venture.   It would be curious to ascertain the exact
annual amount of money brought into those States
from the sale of their children, but the facts are not
officially laid before the public, and a random con-
jecture, or even a shrewd estimate is not now to
the purpose.

In the latter half of the last century, Virginia displayed such an array of talent and statesmanship, of eloquence, of intelligent and manly life, in a noble form as few States with the same population could ever equal; certainly none in America. There were Randolph and Mason, Wythe, Henry, Madison, Jefferson, Marshall, Washington; her very " tobacco " could purchase the peace of New England and New York. Now Virginia is eminent as a nursery of slaves, bred and begotten for the Southern market. Ohio sends abroad the produce of her soil — flour, oxen, and swine; Massachusetts the produce of her mills and manual craft — cottons and woollens, hardware and shoes; while Virginia, chivalrous Virginia, the " Old Dominion," sells in the world's market the produce of her own loins`— men-servants and maidens; her choicest exports are her sons and daughters. She has borne for the nation five Presidents, three of them conspicuous men, famous all over the world; and God knows how many slaves to till the soil of the devouring South. In 1832, it was shown in her legislature that slaves were " all the productive capacity," and " constitute the entire available wealth of Eastern Virginia." The President of William and Mary's College says, " Virginia is a negro-raising State for other States." Thomas Jefferson Randolph pronounced it " one grand menagerie where men are raised for the market like oxen for the shambles."

4

In 1831, it was maintained in her legislature by
Mr. Gholson, that "the owner of land had a rea-
sonable right to its annual profits ; the owner of
orchards to their annual fruits ; the owner of brood-
mares to their products ; and the owner of female
slaves to their increase."

Is any man born a slave ? The Declaration of
Independence says, All men are born " equal ;"
their natural rights " unalienable." It is absurd
to say, a man was born free in Africa, and his
son born a slave in Virginia. The child born in
Africa is made a slave by actual theft and personal violence ; by what other process can he be
made a slave in America ? The fact that his father
was stolen before him makes no difference. By
the law of the United States it is piracy to enslave
a man born in Africa ; by the law of Justice, is it
less piracy to enslave him when born in Baltimore ?

The domestic slave trade is carried on continually in all the great cities of the South ; the capital
of the Union, called after " the Father of his country," is a great slave mart. Droves of slaves,
chained together, may often be seen in the streets
of Washington ; the advertisements of the dealers
are in the journals of that city. There the great
demagogues and the great drovers of slaves meet
together, and one city is common to them all. If
there be degrees in such wrong-doing, it seems
worse to steal a baby in America than a man in

Guinea; worse to keep a gang of women in Virginia breeding children as swine for market, than to steal grown men in Guinea; it is cowardly no less than inhuman. But so long ago as 1829, it was said in the Baltimore Reporter, " Dealing in slaves has become a large business, establishments are made in several places in Maryland, at which they are sold like cattle; these places of deposit are strongly built, and well supplied with iron thumb-screws and gags, and ornamented with cowskins and other whips, often bloody."

The African slave trader perhaps even now, is not unknown at Baltimore or New Orleans, but he is a pirate; he shuffles and hides, goes sneaking and cringes to get along amongst men, while the American slave-trader goes openly to work, advertises " the increase of his female slaves," erects his jail, and when that is insufficient, has those of the nation thrown open for his use, and all the States solemnly pledged to deliver up the fugitives who escape from his hands. He marches his coffles where he will. The laws are on his side, " public sentiment " and the " majesty of the Constitution." He looks in at the door of the Capitol and is not ashamed.

There are mean men engaged in that traffic who " are generally despised even in the slave-holding States," but men of property and standing are also concerned in this trade. Mr. Erwin, the son-in-

law of Mr. Clay, it is said, laid the foundation of a
large fortune by dealing in slaves ; General Jackson was a dealer in slaves and so late as 1811,
bought a coffle and drove them to Louisiana for sale.

In this transfer of slaves the most cruel separation of families takes place.   In the slave-breeding
States it is a common thing to sell a boy or a girl
while the mother is kept as a " Breeder." Does
she complain of the robbery ? — There is the
scourge, there are chains and collars. Will the
husband and father resent the wrong ? — There
are handcuffs and jails ; the law of the United
States, the Constitution, the Army and Navy ; all
the able-bodied men of the free States are legally
bound to come, if need be, and put down the in-
surrection.   Yet, more than fifteen hundred years
ago, a Roman Emperor forbid the separation of
families of slaves, and ordered all which had been
separated to be reunited.   " Who can bear," said
the Emperor to his heathen subjects, " who can
bear that children should be separated from their
parents, sisters from their brothers, wives from
their husbands ? "

In 1836, the Presbyterian Synod of Kentucky
said to the world : " Brothers and sisters, parents
and children, husbands and wives, are torn asunder
and permitted to see each other no more. These
acts are daily occurring in the midst of us.   There

is not a neighborhood where these heart-rending scenes are not displayed. There is not a village or road which does not behold the sad procession of manacled outcasts, whose chains and mournful countenances tell that they are exiled by force from all that their hearts held dear." The affections are proportionally stronger in the Negro than the American; his family his all. The terror of being sold and thus separated from the companions of his sad misfortune, hangs over the slave for ever, at least till too old for service in that way. The most able-minded are of course the most turbulent, the most difficult to manage, and therefore the most commonly sold. But the angel of Death — to them the only angel of Mercy — benignantly visits these poor Ishmaels in the hot swamps of Georgia and Alabama. THOU-GOD-SEEST-ME, were fitting inscription over the spot where the servant thus becomes free from his master and the weary is at rest,

4 *

III.

EFFECTS OF SLAVERY ON INDUSTRY.

LET us examine the Effects of Slavery on Industry in all its forms. In the South manual labor is considered menial and degrading; it is the business of slaves. In the free States the majority work with their hands, counting it the natural business of a man, not a reproach, but a duty and a dignity. Thus in Boston — the richest city of its population in America, and perhaps in the world — out of 19,037 private families in 1845, there were 15,744 who kept no servant, and only 1,069 who had more than one assistant to perform their household labor. In the South the free man shuns labor; "in a slave country every freeman is an aristocrat," and of course labor is avoided by such. Where work is disgraceful, men of spirit will not submit to it. So the high-minded but independent free men are continually getting worse off, or else emigrating out of the slave States into the new free States, — not as the enterprising adventurer goes from New England, because he wants more room, but because his condition is a reproach.

Most of the productive work of the South is done

by slaves. But the slave has no stimulus; the
natural instinct of production is materially checked.
The master has the mouth which consumes, the
slave only the hand which earns. He labors not
for himself, but for another; for another who
continually wrongs him. His aim, therefore, is
to do the least he can get along with. He will
practise no economy; no thrift; he breaks his
tools. He will not think for his master; it is all
hand-work, for he only gives what the master can
force from him, and he cannot conceal; there is
no head-work. There is no invention in the
slave; little among the masters, for their business
is to act on men, not directly on things. This cir-
cumstance may fit the slave-holder for Politics —
of a certain character; it unfits him for the great
operations of productive industry. They and all
labor-saving contrivances come from the North.
In 1846 there were seventy-six patents granted by
the national office for inventions made in fourteen
slave States, with a population of 7,334,431, or one
for each 96,505 persons; at the same time there
were 564 granted to the free States with a population of 9,728,922, or one for each 17,249 persons.
Maryland, by her position, partakes more of the
character of the free States than most of her sisters,
and accordingly made twenty-one inventions —
more than a fourth part of all made in the South.
But Massachusetts had made sixty-two; and

New York, with a population of only 2,428,921, had received two hundred and forty-seven patent-rights — more than three times as many as the whole South. Works which require intelligence and skill require also the hand of the free man. The South can grow timber, it is the North which builds the ships. The South can rear cotton, the free intelligence of the North must weave it into cloth.

In the North the free man acts directly upon things by his own will ; in the South, only through the medium of men reduced to the rank of things, and they act on material objects against their will. Half the moral and intellectual effect of labor is thereby lost ; half the productive power of the labor itself. All the great movements of industry decline where the aristocracy own the bodies of the laboring class. No fertility of soil or loveliness of climate can ever make up for the want of industry, invention and thrift, in the laboring population itself. Agriculture will not thrive as under the free man's hand. Slave labor can only be profitably employed in the coarse operations of field work. It was so in Italy 2000 years ago ; the rich gardens of Latium, Alba, Tuscany, were the work of free men. When their owners were reduced to Slavery by the Roman conqueror, those gardens became only pastures for buffaloes and swine. Only coarse staples, sugar, cotton, rice, corn, tobacco, can be

successfully raised by the slave of America. His
rude tillage impoverishes the soil; the process of
tilth " consists in killing the land." They who will
keep Slavery as a " patriarchal institution," must
adopt the barbarism of the patriarchs, become no-
madic, and wander from the land they have exhausted, to some virgin soil. The free man's fer-
tilizing hand enriches the land the longer he labors.

In Maryland, Virginia, and the Carolinas, the
soil is getting exhausted; the old land less valuable
than the new. In 1787 said Gouverneur Morris,
in the national Convention, " Compare the free regions of the Middle States, where a rich and noble
cultivation marks the prosperity and happiness of
the people, with the misery and poverty which
overspread the barren wastes of Virginia, Maryland, and the other States having slaves. Travel
through the whole Continent, and you behold the
prospect continually varying with the appearance
and disappearance of Slavery. The moment you
leave the Eastern States and enter New York, the
effects of the institution become visible. Passing
through the Jerseys and entering Pennsylvania,
every criterion of superior improvement witnesses
the change. Proceed southwardly, and every step
you take through the great regions of slaves, pre-
sents a desert increasing with the increasing proportion of these wretched beings." At this day,
sixty years later, the contrast is yet more striking,

as will presently appear. Slavery has wrought
after its way. Every tree bears its own fruit.

Slavery discourages the immigration of able but
poor men from the free States. They go elsewhere
to sell their labor; all the Southern States afford
proof of this. The free man from the North will not
put himself and his intelligent industry on a level
with the slave, degraded and despised. In the free
States the farmer buys his land and his cattle; hires
men to aid him in his work — he buys their labor.
Both parties are served — this with labor, that with
employment. There is no degradation, but recip-
rocal gain. In a few years the men who at first
sold their labor will themselves become proprietors,
and hire others desirous of selling their services.
It requires little capital to start with. So the number of proprietors rapidly increases, and the amount
of cultivated land, of wealth, of population, of comfort. In the South the proprietor must also buy
his workmen; the poor man who seeks a market
for his work, not his person, must apply elsewhere.
This cause has long impeded the Agriculture of
the South; it will also hinder the advance of Manufactures. At Lowell the manufacturer builds his
mill, buys his cotton, and reserves a sufficient sum
for his " floating capital; " he hires five hundred
men and women to work his machinery, paying
them from week to week for the labor he has

bought. In South Carolina he must buy his oper-
atives also; five hundred Slaves at $600 each,
amount to $300,000. This additional sum is needed
before a wheel can turn. To start, it requires large
capital; but capital is what is not so easily obtained
in a slave State, where there is no natural stimulus
urging the laboring mass to production. Men of
small capital are kept out of the field; business is
mainly in the hands of the rich; property tends to
accumulate in few hands.

Compare a Slave and a Free State: in the free
population of the former there is less enterprise;
less activity of body and mind; less intelligence;
less production; less comfort, and less welfare. In
the free States an enterprising man whose own hands
are not enough for him to work out his thoughts
with, can trade in human labor, buying men's work
and seeing the result of that work. That is the business of the Merchant-manufacturer in all depart-
ments. In the present state of society both parties
are gainers by the operation. In the South, such a
man must buy the laborers before he can use their
work, but *intelligent* labor he cannot thus buy.

Men are born with different tastes and tenden-
cies — some for agriculture, others for commerce,
navigation, manufactures, for science, letters, the
arts, useful or elegant. The master is able to command the muscles, not to develop the mind. He

directs labor mainly to the coarser operations of husbandry, and makes work monotonous.   Uniformity
of labor involves a great loss.   Political economists
know well the misery which happens to Ireland
from this source — not to mention others and worse.

In Connecticut, every farmer and day-laborer, in
his family or person, is a consumer not only of the
productions of his own farm or handiwork, but
also of tea, coffee, sugar, rice, molasses, salt and
spices ; of cotton, woolen and silk goods, ribbons
and bonnets ; of shoes and hats ; of beds and other
furniture ; of hard-ware, tin-ware and cutlery ;
of crockery and glass ware ; of clocks and jew-
elry ; of books, paper, and the like.   His wants
stimulate the mechanic and the merchant ; they
stimulate him in return, all grow up together ; each
has a market at home, a market continually en-
larging and giving vent to superior wares.   The
young man can turn his hand to the art he likes
best.   Industry, activity, intelligence and comfort
are the result.

In a slave population the reverse of all this takes
place.   The " Southern planter " thinks $20 ad-
equate for the yearly support of a slave.   Add
twenty-five per cent. to his estimate, making the
sum $25 : then the 3,000,000 slaves are consumers
to the amount of $75,000,000 a year.   In 1845 the
annual earnings of the State of Massachusetts were
$114,492,636.   This does not include the improve-

ments made on the soil, nor bridges, railroads, highways, houses, shops, stores and factories that were built — these things form a permanent investment for future years. It cannot reasonably be supposed that, in addition, so large a sum as fourteen per cent. of the annual earnings is saved and laid by. But on that supposition, the 737,699 inhabitants of Massachusetts are consumers to the amount of $100,000,000 a year; that is, $25,000,000, more than four times that number of slaves would consume. The amount of additional energy, comfort and happiness is but poorly indicated even by these figures.

In the present age, Slavery can compete successfully with free labor only under rare circumstances. The population must be sparse; perhaps not exceeding fifty persons to the square mile. But in the nice labor and minute division of employment, in the economy and the improved methods of cultivation, consequent on a dense population, Slavery ceases to be profitable; the slave will not pay for rearing. It must be on a soil extraordinarily fertile, which the barbarous tillage of the slave cannot exhaust. Some of the rich lands of Georgia, Alabama, Louisiana, and Mississippi are of this character. Then it must have the monopoly of some favorite staple, which cannot be produced elsewhere. A combination of those three conditions may render Slavery profitable even at this day, yet by

5

no means so profitable as the work of the free man.
Mr. Rutledge was not far from right in 1787, when
he contended that, in direct taxation, a slave should
pay but one third as much as a freeman, his labor
being only of one third the value of a freeman's.

In the Northern States, the freeman comes directly in contact with the material things which he
wishes to convert to his purpose. To shorten his
labor he makes his head save his hands. He in-
vents machines. The productive capacity of the
free States is extended by their use of Wind, Water and Steam for the purposes of human labor.
That is a solid gain to mankind. Wind-mills, wa-
ter-mills, steam-engines, are the servants of the
North ; Homebred Slaves born in their house, the
increase of fertile heads. These are an important
element in the power and wealth of a nation.
While South Carolina has taken men from Africa,
and made slaves, New England has taken possession
of the Winds, of the Waters ; she has kidnapped
the Merrimack, the Connecticut, the Androscoggin,
the Kennebeck, the Penobscot, and a hundred
smaller streams. She has caught the lakes of New
Hampshire, and holds them in thrall. She has
siezed Fire and Water, joined them with an iron
yoke, and made an army of slaves, powerful, but
pliant. Consider the machinery moved by such
agents in New England, New York, Pennsylvania ;

compare that with the human machines of the South, and which is the better drudge ? The " Patriarchal Institution of Slavery," and the economic institution of Machinery stand side by side,— this representing the nineteenth century before Christ, and that the nineteenth century after Christ. They run for the same goal, though Slavery started first and had the smoother road. It is safe to say, that the machinery of the free States has greater productive ability than the 3,000,000 bondmen of the South. While Slavery continues, the machinery will not appear. Steam-engines and slaves come of a different stock.

The foreign trade of the South consists mainly in the export of the productions of the Farm and the Forest ; the domestic trade in collecting those staples and distributing the articles to be consumed at home. Much of the domestic trade is in the hands of Northern men — though mainly " with Southern principles." The foreign trade is almost wholly in the hands of foreigners, or men from the North, and is conducted by their ships. In the South, little is demanded for home consumption ; so the great staples of Southern production find their market chiefly in the North, or in foreign ports. The shipping is mainly owned by the North. Of the Atlantic States seven have no slaves : Maine, New Hampshire, Massachusetts, Rhode Island, Connecticut,

New York, and New Jersey, in 1846, they, with
Pennsylvania, had 2,160,501 tons of shipping.
In all the slave States which lie on the seaboard,
there are owned but 401,583 tons of shipping. In
1846, the young State of Ohio, two thousand miles
from the sea, had 39,917 tons ; the State of South
Carolina, 32,588. Even Virginia, full of bays and
harbors, had but 53,441 tons. The single district
of the city of New York had 572,522 tons, or
70,939 more than all the Southern States united.

The difference in the internal improvements of
the two sections is quite as remarkable. In general,
the public highways in the slave-holding States are
far inferior to those of the North, both in extent
and character. If the estimates made are correct,
in 1846 there were, omitting the fractions, 5,663
miles of railroad actually in operation in the United
States. In all the slave States together there were
2,090 miles. Taking the cost of such as are described in trustworthy sources, and estimating the
value of those not so described by the general cost
per mile of railroads in the same state, then the slave
States have invested $43,910,183 in this property.
In the free States there were 3,573 miles of railroad,
which had cost $112,914,465. Thus the free States
have 1,483 miles of railroad more than the South,
the value of which is $69,004,282 above the value
of all the railroads of the slave States. The rail-

roads in Pennsylvania have cost $43,426,385; within less than half a million of the value of all the railroads in all the slave States. Maryland, from her position, resembles the free States in many respects. Besides those of this State, all the railroads of the South are worth only $27,717,835, while those of Massachusetts alone have cost $30,341,444, and are now, on the average, five or six per cent. above par. The State of South Carolina has only paid $5,671,452 for her railroad stock. I will not undertake to estimate its present value. Nor need I stop to inquire how many miles of the Southern roads have been planned by Northern skill, paid for by the capital of the free States, and are owned by their citizens!

Let us next consider the increase of the value of the landed property in the Free and the Slave States. In 1798, the value of all the houses and lands in the eight Slave States, that is, Delaware, Maryland, Virginia, North and South Carolina, Georgia, Kentucky and Tennessee, was estimated at $197,742,557; that of the houses and lands in the eight free States — New Hampshire, Vermont, Massachusetts, Connecticut, Rhode Island, New Jersey, New York and Pennsylvania — was $422,235,780. It is not easy to ascertain exactly the value of real property in all these States at this moment. But in 1834 – 6, the government of New

5*

York, and in 1839, that of Virginia, made a new valuation of all the real property in their respective States. In 1798, all the real estate in Virginia, was worth $71,225,127; in 1839, $211,930,538. In 1798, all the real property in the State of New York, was worth $100,380,707; in 1835, $430,751,273. In Virginia, there had been an increase of 197.5 per cent. in forty-one years; in New York, an increase of 329.9 per cent. in thirty-seven years.

For convenience sake, let us suppose each of the eight Southern States has gained as rapidly as Virginia, and each of those eight Northern, in the same ratio with New York — and what follows? In 1798, the real estate in South Carolina was valued at $17,465,013; that of Rhode Island, at $11,066,358. By the above ratios, the real estate in South Carolina was worth $51,958,393 in 1839; and in 1835, that of Rhode Island was worth $47,574,288. Thus the real property in the leading slave State of the Union, with a population of 594,398, was worth but $4,384,105, more than the real property of Rhode Island, with a population of only 108,830. In 1840, the aggregate real property in the city of Boston was valued at $60,424,200, and in 1847, at $97,764,500,— $45,271,120 more than the computed value of all the real estate in South Carolina. In 1798, the value of the aggregate real property of the eight slave States was $197,742,557; of the eight free, $422,235,780; in 1839, by the above ratios, the real estate of the Southern States would be worth $588,289,107, and that of the Northern, $1,715,201,618. Thus the real property of these eight free States would be almost three times more valuable than the eight slave States, yet the free contain but 170,150 square miles, while the slave States contain 212,920. But this, in part, is a matter of calculation only, and liable to some uncertainty as the ratio of Virginia and New York may not represent the increase of any either South or North. Let us come to public and notorious facts.

In 1839, the value of all the annual agricultural products of the South, as valued by the last census, was $312,380,151 ; that of the free States $342,007,446. Yet in the South there were 1,984,866 persons engaged in agriculture, and in the North only 1,735,086, and the South has the advantage of raising tropical productions, which cannot be grown in Europe. The agricultural products of the South which find their way to foreign lands, are mainly cotton, sugar, rice and tobacco. The entire value of these articles raised in the fifteen slave States in that year, was $74,866,310 ; while the agricultural productions of the single State of New York amounted in that year to $108,275,281.

The value of articles manufactured in the South, was $42,178,184 ; in the free States $197,658,040. In the slave States there were, in various manufactories, 246,601 spindles ; in Rhode Island, the smallest of the free States, 518,817. The aggregate annual earnings of all the slave States, was $403,429,718 ; of the free, $658,705,108. The annual earnings of six slave States — North Carolina, South Carolina, Georgia, Alabama, Mississippi, and Louisiana, amount to $189,321,719 ; those of the State of New York to $193,806,433, more than $4,000,000 above the income of six famous States. The annual earnings of Massachusetts alone are more than $9,000,000 greater than the united earning of three slave States, — South Carolina, Georgia, and Florida. The earnings of South Carolina, with her population of 594,398, about equals that of the county of Essex, in Massachusetts, with less than 95,000.

In 1839, in the South there were built houses to the value of $14,421,441 ; and in the North, to the value of $27,496,560. The ships built by the South that year, were valued at $704,289 ; by the North, at $6,301,805.

In 1846, the absolute debt of all the free States, was $109,176,527. The actual productive State-property of those States, including the school fund, was $98,630,285, — leaving the actual indebtedness above their State-property only $10,546,242. The absolute debt of the slave States was $55,948,373 ; their productive State-property, including their school funds, $30,294,428 — leaving their actual indebtedness above their State-property $25,653,945, more than twice the corresponding indebtedness of the North.

Besides this, it must be remembered that in the free States there are 45,569 men engaged in the learned professions, while in the slave States there are but 20,292. In addition to that, in all the free States there are many employed in teaching common schools. Thus, in 1847, in Massachusetts, there were 7,582 engaged in the common schools. In the slave States this class is much smaller. Still more, in all the free States there are many, not ranked in the learned professions, who devote themselves to Science, Literature, and the Fine Arts ; in the South but few. In the South, the female slaves are occupied in hard field-labor, which is almost unheard-of in the free States. Thus the difference in the earnings of the two, great as it is, is not an adequate emblem of the actual difference or productive capacity, or even of the production, in the two sections of the country.

IV.

LET us next consider the Effects of Slavery on the Increase of Numbers, as shown by the great movements of the population in the North and South.

In 1790, the present free States — New England, New York, New Jersey, and Pennsylvania — contained 1,968,455 persons; the slave States 1,961,372. In 1840 the same slave States, Delaware, Maryland, Virginia, North Carolina, South Carolina, Georgia, Kentucky — contained 5,479,860; the same free States, 6,767,082. In 50 years those slave States had increased 179 per cent.; those free States 243 per cent., or with 64 per cent. greater rapidity.

In 1790 the entire population of all the slave States was 1,961,372; in 1840, including the new slave States, 7,334,431; while the population of the free States — including the new ones — was 9,728,922. The slave States had increased 279 per cent.; the free, 394, the latter increasing with a rapidity 115 per cent. greater than the former.

In 1810 the new slave States, — Louisiana, Mississippi, Alabama, Arkansas, Tennessee, Missouri, and Kentucky — contained 805,991 persons; the new free States — Ohio, Indiana, Illinois, Michigan — contained but 272,324. But in 1840 those new slave States, with the addition of Florida, contained 3,409,132, while the population of the new free States — with the addition of Wisconsin and Iowa — contained 2,967,840. In 50 years the new slave States had increased 323 per cent., and the new free States 1,090 per cent.

In 1790, the whole free population of the present free States was 1,930,125; the free population of the present slave States and territories was 1,394,847. The difference in the number of free persons in the North and South was only 535,278. But in 1840 the free population of the free States and Territories was 9,727,893; the free population of the slave States and territories only 4,848,105; the difference between the two was 4,879,788. In 50 years the free persons in the slave States had increased 247 per cent.; the free persons of the free States 404 per cent. It is true something has been added to the North by immigrations from abroad, but the accessions which the South has received by the purchase of Louisiana and Florida, by the immigration of enterprising men from the North, and by the importation of slaves, is perhaps more than adequate to balance the northern increase by foreign immigration.

The Southern States have great advantages over the Northern, in soil, climate, and situation ; they have a monopoly of the tropical productions so greatly sought by all northern nations ; they have superior facilities for the acquisition of wealth, and through that for the rapid increase of population. In some countries the advance of both is retarded by oppressive legislation. Of this the South cannot complain, as it will by and by appear. The new land lay nearer to the old Southern States than the old free States, and that not " infested with Indians " to the same extent with the soil since conquered and colonized by the emigrants from the Northern States. The difference of the increase of the two in wealth and numbers, is to be ascribed, therefore, to the different institutions of the two sections of the land.

V.

LET us now look at the Effects of Slavery on the intellectual, moral and religious Development of the People. The effect on the intellectual, moral and religious condition of the SLAVE is easily understood. He is only continued in Slavery by restraining him from the civilization of mankind in this age. His mind, conscience, soul — all his nobler powers — must be kept in a state of inferior development, otherwise he will not be a slave in the nineteenth century, and in the United States. In comparison with the intellectual culture of their masters the slaves are a mass of Barbarians, still more emphatically, when compared with the free institutions of the North; they are Savages. This is not a mere matter of inference, the fact is substantiated by the notorious testimony of slave-holders themselves. In 1834 the Synod of South Carolina and Georgia reported that the slaves " may justly be considered the Heathen of this country, and will bear comparison with the Heathen of any

6

part of the world." "They are destitute of the
privileges of the Gospel, and ever will be under the
present state of things." In all the slave Sates,
says the Synod, there are "not twelve men exclusively devoted to the religious instruction of the
Negroes." Of the regular ministers "but a very
small portion pay any attention to them." "We
know of but five churches in the slave-holding States
built exclusively for their use," and "there is no
sufficient room for them in the white churches for
their accommodation." "They are unable to read,
as custom, or law, and generally both, prohibit
their instruction. They have no Bible — no family altars; and when in affliction, sickness, or death,
they have no minister to address to them the con-
solations of the Gospel, nor to bury them with
solemn and appropriate services." They may
sometimes be petted and caressed as children and
toys, they are never treated as men.

"Heathenism," says another Southern authority,
"is as real in the slave States as in the South Sea
Islands." "Chastity is no virtue among them [the
slaves] ; its violation neither injures female character in their own estimation nor that of their mis-
tress." Where there is no marriage recognized by
the State or Church as legal and permanent between
slaves ; where the female slave is wholly in her
master's power — how can it be otherwise? Said
the Roman proverb, " Nothing is unlawful for the

master to his slave." When men are counted as things, instruments of husbandry, separable limbs of the master, and retained in subjugation by external force and the prohibition of all manly culture, the effect of Slavery on its victim is so obvious that no more need be said thereof.

The effect of Slavery on the intellectual, moral, and religious condition of the FREE POPULATION of the South, is not so obvious perhaps at first sight. But a comparison with the free States will render that also plain.

All attempts at the improvement of the humbler and more exposed portions of society, the perishing and dangerous classes thereof, originate in the free States. It is there that men originate societies for the Reform of Prisons, the Prevention of Crime, Pauperism, Intemperance, Licentiousness and Ignorance. There spring up Education-Societies, Bible - Societies, Peace - Societies, Societies for teaching Christianity in foreign and barbarous lands. There too are the learned and philosophical societies, for the study of Science, Letters, and Art. Whence come the men of superior education who occupy the Pulpits, exercise the professions of Law and Medicine, or fill the chairs of the Professors in the Colleges of the Union? Almost all from the North, from the free States. There is preaching every where. But search the whole

Southern States for the last seven-and-forty years,
and it were hard to show a single preacher of any
eminence in any pulpit of a slave-holding State ; a
single clergyman remarkable for ability in his calling,
for great ideas, for eloquence, elsewhere so cheap
— or even for learning ! Even Expositions and
Commentaries on the Bible, the most common cler-
ical productions, are the work of the North alone.

Whence come the distinguished authors of Amer-
ica ? the Poets — Bryant, Longfellow, Whittier ;
Historians — Sparks, Prescott, Bancroft ; Jurists —
Parsons, Wheaton, Story, Kent ! Whence Irving,
Channing, Emerson ; — whence all the scientific
men, the men of thought, who represent the Na-
tion's loftier consciousness ? All from the free
States ; north of Mason and Dixon's line !

Few works of any literary or scientific value
have been written in this country in any of the
slave States ; few even get reprinted there. Compare the works which issue from the press of New
Orleans, Savannah, Charleston, Norfolk, Baltimore,
with such as come from Philadelphia, NewYork,
and Boston — even from Lowell and Cincinnati ;
compare but the Booksellers' stock in those several
cities, and the difference between the cultivation of
the more educated classes of the South and North
is apparent at a glance.

But leaving general considerations of this sort, let

us look at facts. In 1671, Sir William Berkely, Governor of Virginia, said, " I thank God that there are no free schools nor printing presses, [in Virginia] and I hope we shall not have them these hundred years." In 1840, in the fifteen slave States and territories, there were at the various primary schools 201,085 scholars; at the various primary schools of the free States 1,626,028. The State of Ohio alone, had 218,609 scholars at her primary schools, 17,524 more than all the fifteen slave States. South Carolina had 12,520 such scholars, and Rhode Island 17,355. New York alone had 502,367.

In the higher schools there were in the South, 35,935 " scholars at the public charge," as they are called in the census; in the North, 432,388 similar scholars. Virginia, the largest of the slave States had 9,791 such scholars; Rhode Island, the smallest of the free States 10,749. Massachusetts alone had 158,351, more than four times as many as all the slave States.

In the slave States, at academies and grammar schools, there were 52,906 scholars; in the free States, 97,174. But the difference in numbers here does not represent the difference of fact, for most of the academies and grammar schools of the South are inferior to the " schools at public charge " of the North; far inferior to the better portion of the Northern " District Schools."

In 1840 there were at the various Colleges in the

6*

South, 7,106 pupils, and in the free States, 8,927. Here too, the figures fail to indicate the actual dif- ference in the numbers of such as receive a superior education; for the greater part of the eighty-seven " Universities and Colleges " of the South are much inferior to the better Academies and High Schools of the North.

In the libraries of all the Universities and Col- leges of the South there are 223,416 volumes; in those of the North, 593,897. The libraries of the Theological schools of the South contain 22,800 volumes; those of the North, 102,080. The dif- ference in the character and value of these volumes does not appear in the returns.

In the slave States there are 1,368,325 free white children between the ages of five and twenty; in the free States, 3,536,689 such children. In the slave States, at schools and colleges, there are 301,172 pupils; in the free States, 2,212,444 pupils, at schools or colleges. Thus, in the slave States, out of twenty-five free white children between five and twenty, there are not quite five at any school or college; while out of twenty-five such children in the free States, there are more than fifteen at school or college.

In the slave States, of the free white population that is over twenty years of age, there is almost one tenth part that are unable to read and write; while in the free States there is not quite one in one hundred and fifty-six who is deficient to that degree.

In New England there are but few born therein and more than twenty years of age, who are unable to read and write ; but many foreigners arrive there with no education, and thus swell the number of the illiterate, and diminish the apparent effect of her free institutions. The South has few such emigrants ; the ignorance of the Southern States therefore is to be ascribed to other causes. The Northern men who settle in the slave-holding States, have perhaps about the average culture of the North, and more than that of the South. The South therefore gains educationally from immigration as the North loses.

Among the Northern States Connecticut, and among the Southern States, South Carolina, are to a great degree free from disturbing influences of this character. A comparison between the two will show the relative effects of the respective institutions of the North and South. In Connecticut, there are 163,843 free persons over twenty years of age ; in South Carolina but 111,663. In Connecticut, there are but 526 persons over twenty who are unable to read and write, while in South Carolina there are 20,615 free white persons over twenty years of age unable to read and write. In South Carolina, out of each 626 free whites more than twenty years of age, there are more than 58 wholly unable to read or write; out of that number of such persons in Connecticut, not quite two! More than the sixth part of the adult freemen of South Carolina are unable to read the vote which will, be deposited at the next election. It is but fair to infer that at least one third of the adults of South Carolina, if not of much of the South, are unable to read and understand even a newspaper. Indeed, in one of the slave States, this is not a matter of mere inference, for in 1837 Gov. Clarke, of Kentucky, declared, in his message to the legislature, that "one third of the adult population were unable to write their names;" yet Kentucky has a "school-fund," valued at $1,221,819, while South Carolina has none.

One sign of this want of ability even to read, in the slave States, is too striking to be passed by. The staple reading of the least cultivated Americans is the newspapers, one of the lowest forms of literature, though one of the most powerful, read even by men who read nothing else. In the slave States there are published but 377 newspapers, and in the free 1,135. These numbers do not express the entire difference in the case, for as a general rule the circulation of the Southern newspapers is 50 to 75 per cent. less than that of the North. Suppose, however, that each Southern newspaper has two thirds the circulation of a Northern journal, we have then but 225 newspapers for the slave

States ! The more valuable journals — the monthlies and quarterlies — are published almost entirely in the free States.

The number of Churches, the number and character of the clergy who labor for these churches, are other measures of the intellectual and moral condition of the people. The scientific character of the Southern clergy has been already touched on. Let us compare the more external facts.

In 1830, South Carolina had a population of 581,185 souls; Connecticut 297,675. In 1836, South Carolina had 364 ministers; Connecticut 498.

In 1834, there were in the slave States but 82,532 scholars in . the Sunday schools ; in the free States 504,835 ; in the single State of New York, 161,768.

A cause which keeps 3,000,000 men in bondage in America and the nineteenth century, has more subtle influences than those just now considered. It not only prevents the extension of education among the people, but affects the doctrines taught them, even the doctrines taught in the name of God. Christianity is nominally the public Religion of America ; not of the Government, which extends protection alike to all modes of worship, of the Indian, the Mormon, and the Jew, but of the people. I will not touch the doctrines of the sects, in which Christian differs from Christian, but come to what is general among Christians — a part of the universal Religion implied also in Human Nature itself. All sects, as such, theoretically agree that the most important *practical* doctrine of Christianity is LOVE TO MEN ; to all men, of all ages, races, and conditions. As the Christian idea of God rises far above the Heathen or Hebrew conception thereof, so the Christian idea of man's relation to man far transcends the popular notions of human duty which formerly had prevailed. God is " OUR FATHER," the God of Love ; Man OUR BROTHER, whom we are bound to love as ourselves, and treat as we would be treated. Christian Piety, or Love of God, involves Christian Morality, or Love of Man.

I lay aside the peculiar theoretical doctrines of the sects, that are preached everywhere, and ask : Can the Christian relations of human Brotherhood, the Christian duty of Love to Men, be practically preached in the Slave States ? I only publish an open secret in saying it is impossible. The forms of Christianity may be preached, not its piety, not its morality, not even its philosophy, or its history. If a man holds slaves in practice and justifies the deed in theory, how can he address an audience of slaveholders and teach them the duty of loving others as themselves ? He cannot consistently teach that doctrine, nor they consistently hear.

The doctrines of the public religion are always modified by national habits, history, institutions,

and ideas. Christianity, as taught in New England,
has modifications unknown in Old England.   The
great national and peculiar ideas of America — of
which I shall soon speak — are among the truths of
Christianity.   We began our national career by declaring all men born with equal rights.   In such a
people we might look for a better and more universal development of Christianity, than in a nation which knows no unalienable rights, or equality
of all men, but robs the many of their rights, to
squander privileges on the few.

In some lands Monarchy, Aristocracy, Prelacy,
appear in the public teaching as parts of Christianity.   In America it is not so.   But it is taught that
Slavery is an ordinance of God, — justified by
Christianity.   Thus as the public Religion is elsewhere made to subserve the private purposes of
Kings, Nobles, Priests — so here is it made to
prove the justice of holding men in bondage.
There are no chains like those wrought in the
name of God, and welded upon their victim by the
teachers of Religion.

Most of the churches in the United States exercise the power of excluding a man from their communion for such offences as they see fit; for any
unpopular breach of the moral law; — for murder,
robbery, theft, public drunkenness, seduction, licentiousness, for heresy.   Even dancing is an offence

for which the churches sometimes *deal* with their children. But, with the exception of the Quakers and the United Brethren, no religious bodies in the United States now regard slave-holding or slave-dealing as an ecclesiastical offence. Church-members and clergymen are owners of slaves. Even churches themselves in some instances 'have, in their corporate capacity, been owners of men. In Turkey, when a man becomes a Mahometan, he ceases to be a slave. But in America a clergyman may own a member of his own church, beat him, sell him, and grow rich on " the increase of his female slaves."

Few productions of the Southern clergy find their way to the North. Conspicuous among those few are sermons in defence of Slavery ; attempts to show that if Christ were now on earth he might consistently hold property in men !

The teachings of the Southern pulpit become more and more favorable to Slavery. Oppressed, America promulgated the Theory of Freedom ; — free, she established the practice of Oppression. In 1780 the Methodist Episcopal Church declared " Slavery is contrary to the laws of God," and " hurtful to society ;" in 1784 it refused to admit slave-holders to its communion — passing a vote to exclude all such. But in 1836 the General Conference voted " not to interfere in the civil and political relations between master and slave," and exhorted its minis-

ters "to abstain from all abolition movements."
The General Conference has since declared that
American Slavery "is not a moral evil." The
Conference of South Carolina has made a similar
declaration.

In 1794 the Presbyterian Church added a note
to the eighth commandment, bringing Slavery under that prohibition, declaring it manstealing and a
sin. Yet, though often entreated, it did not excom-
municate for that offence. In 1816, by a public de-
cree, the note was erased. Numerous Presbyteries
and Synods have passed resolutions like these:
"Slavery is not opposed to the will of God;"
"It is compatible with the most fraternal regard to
the best good of those servants whom God may
have committed to our charge." Even the Catholic Church in the United States forms no exception
to the general rule. The late lamented Dr. England, the Catholic Bishop of Charleston, South
Carolina, undertook in public to prove that the
Catholic Church had always been the uncompro-
mising friend of slaveholding, not defending the
slaves' Right, but the usurped Privilege of the masters. What a difference between the present Christian Pope of Rome, and the Bishop of a democratic
State in a Christian Republic!

It has been currently taught in the most popular
churches of the land, that Slavery is a "Christian
institution,' sustained by the Apostles, and sanc-

7

tioned by Christ himself. None of the theological
parties has been so little connected with Slavery
as the Unitarians — perhaps from the smallness
of the sect itself, and its northern latitude — but,
for years, one of its vice-presidents was a slave-
holder.

While the Southern churches teach that Slavery
is Christian, the Northern join in the belief. Here
and there a few voices in the North have been
lifted up against it; seldom an eminent voice in an
eminent place, then to be met with obloquy and
shame. Almost all the churches in the land seem
joined in opposing such as draw public attention to
the fact that a Christian Republic holds millions of
men in bondage. Not long since a clergyman of
the South, who boasted that he owned thirty slaves,
and " would wade knee-deep in blood " to defend
his right to them, was received by the Northern
churches, and as himself has said, " invited on
every hand to pulpits," with no rebuke, but only
welcome from the large and powerful denomination to which he belonged. He returned, as he
says, " leaving the hot-beds of abolitionism, without
having been once foiled. God be praised for sus-
taining me. I give Him all the glory, for without
Him I am nothing." Even in Boston there is a
church of the same denomination, in which no
colored man is allowed to purchase a seat. Colored
men at the North are excluded from colleges and

high schools, from theological seminaries and from respectable churches — even from the Town Hall and the Ballot.   Doctrines and outward deeds are but signs of Sentiments and Ideas which rule the life.

The sons of the North, when they settle in the South, as merchants, ministers, lawyers, planters, when they stand in the congress of the nation ; when they fill important offices in the federal government — what testimony do they bear to the declaration that " all men are created equal ? "   I should blush to refresh your memories with Northern Shame.

If the clergy find Slavery " ordained " in the Bible, and established amongst the " Christian institutions," did not the laymen first find it in the Bible of Rousseau ?   Important men at the South have taught that Slavery is " a moral and humane institution, productive of the greatest political and social advantages ;" " the corner stone of our republican edifice :" " It is the most sure and stable edifice for free institutions in the world."   The doctrine that " all men are created equal " in Rights is declared " ridiculously absurd."   Democratic Mr. Calhoun declares that where " common labor is performed by members of the political community a dangerous element is obviously introduced into the body politic."   A Pagan had taught it two thousand years before.

Thus powerful is the influence of Slavery in its action on the intellectual, moral and religious development of the people at the South; thus subtly does it steal upon the North. As one of your most illustrious citizens, old but not idle, has said, the Spirit of Slavery " has crept into the philosophical chairs of the Schools. Its cloven foot has ascended the pulpits of the churches. Professors of colleges teach it as a lesson of morals ; ministers of the gospel seek and profess to find sanctions for it in the Word of God."

The effect of Slavery on the industrial, numerical, intellectual and moral developments of the people may be best shown by a comparison of the condition and history of the two largest States, one Slave, the other Free. Virginia contains more than 64,000 square miles, or 13,370 more than England. The climate is delightful. The State is intersected by " the finest bay in the world ; " watered by long and abundant rivers, this inviting navigation, and allowing numerous and easy communications with the interior ; that waiting to turn the wheels of the manufacturer, to weave and spin. The soil is rich in minerals. Iron, Lead and Limestone are abundant. Nitre is found in her caverns. Salt abounds on the Great Kenawha and the Holston. Fields of coal, anthracite and bituminous, are numerous, rich, and of easy access. The soil is fertile, the

sky genial, the air salubrious. She is the oldest
State in the Union; long the most important in
wealth, population and political power. The noble
array of talent and virtue found there in the last
century has already been mentioned. Abundantly
blessed with bays, harbors, rivers, mines, no State
in the Union had such natural advantages as Virginia in 1790. New York has 49,000 square miles,
and was settled somewhat later than Virginia, and
under circumstances less propitious. Numerous
causes retarded her growth before the Revolution.
Though favored with an excellent harbor, she has
but one natural channel of communication with the
interior. In 1790 Virginia contained 748,348 inhabitants; New York but 340,120. In 1840 Virginia had 1,239,797; New York 2,428,921, and in
1845, 2,604,495. In fifty years Virginia had not
doubled her population, while New York had increased more than fourfold. In 1790, Virginia
had more than eleven inhabitants to each square
mile, and New York not quite eight; but in 1840,
Virginia had only nineteen, and New York fifty-
three persons to the square mile. In 1798, the
houses and lands of Virginia were valued at
$71,225,127, those of New York at $100,380,707;
in 1839 the real estate in Virginia was worth but
$211,930,538, while that of New York had in-
creased to $430,751,273. In 1840 the annual
earnings of Virginia were $76,769,032; of New
7*

York $193,806,433. The population of New York is not quite double that of Virginia, but her annual earnings nearly three times as great. In 1840, at her various colleges and schools, Virginia had 57,302 scholars, and also 58,787 adult free whites unable to read and write — 1,484 more than the entire number of her children at school or college. New York had 44,452 illiterate adults, and 565,442 children at school or college. Besides that, in Virginia there were 448,987 slaves, with no literary culture at all, shut out from communication with the intelligence of the age. In 1844, in New York, 709,156 children, between four and sixteen, attended the common public schools of the State, and the common school libraries contained over a million of volumes; while in Virginia there were over 100,000 free white children between four and sixteen, who attended no school at all, perpetual vagrants from learning, year out and year in. Shall it always be so ? The effect follows the cause. A man loses half his manhood, by Slavery, said Homer, and it is as true of a State as a man.

VI.

I now call your attention to the Influence of
Slavery on Law and Politics, its local effect on the
Slave States in special, its general effect on the
Politics of the Union.

In the settlement of America only the People
came over. Nobility and Royalty did not migrate.
The People, the Third Estate, of course brought
the Institutions and Laws of their native land —
these are the National Habits, so to say. But they
brought also political Sentiments and Ideas not
represented by the Institutions or Laws; Sentiments
and Ideas hostile thereto, and which could not be
made real in England, but were destined — as are
all such Ideas — to form Institutions and make
Laws in their own image. There are three such
political Ideas which have already found a theoretical expression, and have more or less been made
Facts and become incarnate in Institutions and
Laws. These are, first, the Idea, that in virtue of

his manhood, EACH MAN HAS UNALIENABLE RIGHTS, not derived from men or revocable thereby, but derived only from God; second, that in respect to these Rights ALL MEN ARE CREATED EQUAL; third, that THE SOLE DESIGN OF POLITICAL GOVERNMENT IS TO PLACE EVERY MAN IN THE ENTIRE POSSESSION OF ALL HIS UNALIENABLE RIGHTS.

The Priesthood, Nobility, Royalty, did not share these Ideas — nor the Sentiments which led to them. These Ideas were of the people; they must form a Democracy, THE GOVERNMENT OF ALL, FOR ALL AND BY ALL — a Commonwealth with no privileged class — a State without Nobles or Kings, a Church without Prelate or Priest.

These Ideas, in becoming facts and founding political Institutions to represent themselves, modified also the ancient and Common Law. "The Laws of England," said Sir John Fortescue, in the fifteenth century, "the Laws of England favor Liberty in every case;" "let him who favors not liberty be judged impious and cruel." After the national and solemn expression of the above Democratic Ideas, the laws must favor liberty yet more, and new Institutions likewise come into being. Accordingly, in the free States of the North, where these Ideas have always had the fullest practical exposition, ever since the Revolution there has been a continual advance in legislation — laws becoming more humane, universal principles getting established, and traditional exceptions becoming annulled. In Law — the theory of these Ideas — so far as expressed in Institutions and habits — and in Society — the practice thereof, so far as they have passed into actual life, there is a constant levelling upward ; the low are raised — the Slave, the Servant, the Non-Freeholder ; the lofty not degraded.. In the constitutions of nearly all the free States it is distinctly stated that ALL MEN ARE CREATED EQUAL IN RIGHTS, and in all it is implied. They all are advancing towards a realization of that Idea—slowly, but constantly. They have lost none of the Justice embodied in the Common Law of their ancestors — but gained new Justice, and embodied it in their own forms.

This Idea of the natural equality of all men in Rights, is inconsistent with Slavery ; accordingly it is expressed in the constitution of but one slave State — Virginia. It is consistently rejected by the politicians of the South. This difference of Ideas must appear in all the Institutions of the North and South, and produce continual and conflicting modifications of the Common Law of England, which they both inherit ; if the one Idea adds Justice thereto, the other takes it away.

Now among the institutions inherited from England were the Trial by a Jury of twelve men in all matters affecting liberty and life ; the Presump-

tion in favor of life, liberty and innocence ; the
Right of every man under restraint to have a legal
reason publicly shown for his confinement, by a
writ of Habeas Corpus. The form of the latter
is indeed modern, but its substance old, and of un-
certain date. These three have long been regarded as the great Safeguards of public justice, and in
the legislation of the free States remain undisturbed
in their beneficent action, extending to every person therein. In the slave States the whole class of
Bondmen is in fact mainly deprived of them all.

By the customs of England and her Law, while
Villanage obtained there, the rule was that the child
followed the condition of its Father : *Filius sequitur
Patrem.* Hence the issue of a freeman, though
born of a servile mother, was always free. In virtue of this maxim, and the legal Presumption in
favor of Liberty, a presumption extending to all
classes of men, the child of a female slave, which
was born out of wedlock, was of course free. It
was possible the father was a free man. The child
gained nothing but existence from his unknown
father, and the Law would not make that a curse.
The child of a slave father, but born before the father
was proved a slave, retained his freedom forever.

If a freeman married a female slave, she became
free during the life of her husband, and the children of course were free.

The slave, under certain circumstances, could

possess property, acquired by devise, by gift, or other means. It was so as a general rule through all the North of Europe; the more cruel maxims of the Roman slave-code never prevailed with the Teutonic race.

The slave could make a contract with his lord, binding as that between peer and peer. He could in his own name bring an action against any one; in some cases even against his master. He could, in all cases and in his own name, demand a Trial by Jury in a court of record, to determine if he were born a slave, or free. To determine against him, it was necessary not only to show in general that he was a slave, but that he was the slave of some one person in special. If it was simply shown that the man was a slave, but was not shown to the Jury's satisfaction that he was the slave of the particular man who claimed him, the slave received his freedom at once, as one derelict by his master, and if legally claimed by nobody, he naturally belonged to himself.

He could be a witness in any court even when his master was an adverse party; though not possessed of all the privileges of a citizen — *legalis Homo* — not admitted to hold office or serve on a jury, yet he could testify on oath even in criminal cases, as any other man.

If a slave ran away, and the master for one year neglected to pursue him with public outcry and

prosecution of his claim, the slave was free by adverse possession of himself.   While he was in
flight, and in actual possession of freedom, the
master could not seize on his children or on his
possessions.   He must legally possess the Princi-
pal, the Substance, before he could touch the Subordinate and Accident thereof.   Did the slave flee
to another borough or shire, a jury of that place, —
except in certain cases, when the trial must take
place in another county,— must not only convict him
as a slave before the master could recover his body,
but must convict him of being the slave of that special claimant.

If a slave took orders in the Church, or became
a monk, he was free from his master, though this
was an exception to the law in most Catholic countries.   If violence were offered to a female slave
by her master, she had redress as a free woman.
Slaves had all the personal rights of freemen except in regard to their own respective masters, and
in some cases even then.   There was no hindrance
to manumission.

In America the laws relating to Slavery are in
many respects more severe than the English laws,
since the Norman conquest, respecting villains —
regardant or *in gross.*   The child's condition follows that of the mother.   This American departure
from the Common Law was early made by statute,

and the opposite maxim, the rule of the Civil Law, extended over the slave States ; — *Partus sequitur Ventrem.* Illegitimate children of female slaves were of course slaves forever, though the father was free. But for this alteration, many thousands of men now slaves would have been free.

Contrary to the old Common Law of England, but in obedience to the Roman code, the American slave, in law is regarded merely as a THING ; "doomed," as Judge Ruffin, of North Carolina, sorrowfully declares, " to live without knowledge and without the capacity to make anything his own, and to toil that another may reap the fruits." In some of the slave States Trial by Jury is allowed to him in all capital cases ; sometimes with the concurrence of a grand jury, sometimes without. Sometimes he is allowed to challenge the jurors " for cause," though not peremptorily. But in South Carolina, Virginia, and Louisiana, the slave is not allowed a jury trial, even when his life is in peril. In some others he has the protection of a jury when arraigned for inferior offences. But in every slave State he may be beaten to the extent of " thirty-nine lashes well laid on," without the verdict of a jury, but by the decision of a body of justices of the peace, varying in number from two to five. In all cases he is tried by men who regard him only as a thing, never by a jury of HIS PEERS — not even by

8

a mixed jury of slave-holders and slaves. Some
States have made humane provisions to guard
against popular excitement, removing the trial to
another county; now and then humane decisions
are made in their favor by just men. But these are
exceptional spots of humanity amidst the general
gloom of the slave-code. There is some difference
in the legislation of the several States, justifying the
remark long ago made in Europe, that the condition of slaves was mildest in the North — hardest
in the South.

Since the slave is a Thing, he is not allowed his
oath; sometimes he may give legal evidence for or
against another slave, though without any form of
solemn affirmation. There are laws in all the slave
States designed to restrain the master from excessive
cruelty, still they afford but incomplete protection
to the slave; he cannot bring an action against the
oppressor in his own name — for, as a THING, he
has no Rights. No slave, free negro, or mulatto to
the fourth degree of descent is allowed to testify
against a white man; as if this were not enough
in South Carolina and Louisiana, if a slave is
injured or killed when only one white person is
present — and the presumption of guilt fall on the
one white man, he is allowed by statute "to clear
or exculpate himself by his own oath." This law
is worse than the code of the Romans, " whose

history was written in the blood of vanquished nations."

The slave has no legal right of self-defence against his master's assault and battery ; the female none against brutal violation. The law of Georgia directs that "if any slave shall presume to strike any white man, such slave shall, for the first offence, suffer such punishment as the justice or justices shall see fit, not extending to life or limb; and, for the second offence, suffer death." In South Carolina, on his owner's account, he is allowed to strike even a white man, and the offence is capital only when twice repeated. In Kentucky, the penalty is less severe, but applied to free men of color as well as slaves.

A slave cannot be party to a civil suit. Indeed, when his condition is doubtful, he may apply to a court, and the court authorize some man to act as "guardian," and bring an action in the slave's behalf, and have investigation made of his servitude. But the burthen of proof remains on the slave's shoulders — to show that he is free. The presumption that he is a slave — *Presumptio malæ Partis* — prevails in all the South except North Carolina, — where the slave-code is perhaps more humane than elsewhere, — and is thus declared by statute in South Carolina and Georgia : "It shall always be pre-

sumed that every negro, Indian, mulatto and mes-
tizo is a slave." No adverse possession of himself, however long, makes a negro free, or his
offspring born while he is in that state. In Mississippi, every negro, or mulatto, not able to prove
that he is free, may be sold by order of court, as a
slave forever. If an applicant for freedom is cast
in his suit, the court is "fully empowered to inflict
such punishment not extending to life and limb, as
they should think fit;" the "guardian" shall pay
the costs; and in South Carolina, double those costs
with damages to the owner of the slave. In Virginia, such a guardian, if defeated in his application, may be fined $100. In such a trial in Mary-
land, the master is allowed to challenge peremptorily twelve jurors. How difficult to find a
"guardian" willing to incur the risk; how more
than difficult to secure justice when a negro is
wrongfully claimed as a slave! Yet notwithstanding the general spirit displayed by such legislation,
some decisions have been made in the Southern
States remarkable for the nicety of legal distinction and the exactness of their justice even to the
slave.

Since the slave is a Thing in many States, a con-
ditional contract which the master has solemnly
made with a slave, is not binding on the master,
even after the slave has fulfilled the contract in
spirit and letter. This is notoriously the law in

South Carolina, and even in Virginia. A contract made with a spade or a mule binds no man — with a slave no more ; the court cannot proceed to " enforce a contract between master and slave, even though the contract should be fully complied with on the part of the slave." This is a departure from the Common Law of England, and even from the customs of the Saxons and Germans.

The Common Law of England jealously defends the little property of the slave ; — his *Peculium*. By the common law of Villanage, in England and Germany, he could acquire property as it was said above, and could transmit it to his heirs. Something of the sort was allowed even at Rome. But in all thesl ave States this is strictly forbidden. A slave cannot hold property solemnly devised to him by testament, even by that of his master. This provision, enforced by statute in Virginia, North Carolina, South Carolina, Georgia, Mississippi, Kentucky, and Tennessee, and perhaps all the Slave States, is more rigorous even than the black codes of the Spanish and Portuguese colonies.

By the Common Law, the marriage of a slave was sacred as that of a peer of the realm. The Customs of Turkey, regard it as inviolable. Even the Roman code respected that, and the Common Law, by making marriage a sacrament rendered

8*

it perpetual. " Neither bond nor free may be separated from the sacraments of the church," said the Decretal of Gregory, " the marriages among slaves must not be hindered, and though contracted against their master's will, ought not, on that account, to be dissolved." But in the American law, the slave cannot contract marriage. In North Carolina, no marriage is legal between whites and persons of color, including in the latter term all descended from a negro to the fourth generation.

In some States it is a penal offence to teach slaves the elements of common learning. By the recent code of Virginia, any one who undertakes to teach reading or writing to slaves, or even free colored persons, may be fined from $10 to $100. The same is forbidden in Georgia. In Alabama, the punishment is a fine from $250 to $500; in Mississippi, imprisonment for one year. Lousiana forbids the teaching of slaves to read or write, and prohibits any one from using language in public discourse or private conversation, having a tendency to produce discontent among the free colored population. The latter offence is punishable " with imprisonment or death at the discretion of the court." This antipathy to the education of the colored race, extends even to the free States. It is not unknown in New England. The State of Ohio, established schools in 1829 for " the *white* youth of every class and grade without distinction.''

According to the alleged precept of Mahomet, slaves are supposed to be bound by feebler, social and civil obligations than free men, and thus common offences receive but half the punishment of the free. Such it is said is the Common Law of Mahometans in Turkey, and the East. In Virginia there are six capital offences for a freeman, seventy-one for a slave. In Mississippi there are thirty-eight offences for which a slave must be punished with death, — not one of which is a capital crime in a free white man. In some States the law is milder, but in none does the Christian Republican of Anglo Saxon descent imitate the humanity of the Mussulman, and legally favor the weaker part — correcting slaves as the children of the State.

Many offences for which a slave is severely punished, are not wrongs by Nature, sins against the Universal and Divine Law, but only crimes by Statute. Thus in Mississippi, if a slave be found " fire-hunting " he is punishable " with thirty-nine lashes, well laid on his bare back." In the same State, if a slave be found out of the limits of the town, or off the plantation where he usually works, " any one may apprehend and punish him with whipping on the bare back, not exceeding

twenty lashes." If he refuses to submit to the
examination of any white person, "such white
person may apprehend and moderately correct
him, and if he shall assault and strike such white
person, he may be lawfully killed." Louisiana has
a similar law, and also punishes any slave or free
colored person exercising the functions of a minister
of the Gospel, with thirty-nine lashes. In Virginia
a slave or free colored person may be beaten with
twenty lashes for being found at any school for
teaching reading and writing. In South Carolina
he is forbidden to wear any but the coarsest
garments.

The Roman code allowed emancipation; the
Customs of England and Germany favored it. The
Christian church often favored and recommended it.
In the Roman Empire, the advance of humanity
continually rendered it easy and common. A slave
sick, and derelict of his master, recovering, claimed
legally his freedom for salvage of himself. But
in America the laws constantly throw obstacles
in its way. In South Carolina, Georgia, Alabama,
and Mississippi no man can emancipate any slave,
except by authority of the Legislature, granted by
a special enactment conveying the power. In
Georgia, a Will, setting free a slave, is so far null
and void, and any person attempting to execute
it, shall be fined $1000. In Kentucky, Missouri,

Virginia, Maryland, it is less difficult; but even
there no man is allowed to emancipate a slave to
the prejudice of his creditors; — or in Virginia,
Mississippi and Kentucky, to the lessening of his
widow's dower, the Common Law, favors three
things — Life, Liberty and Dower; — the law of
these three States sacrifices the Liberty of Slaves
to the Dower of a widow. Emancipation must
be made with most formal and technical minute-
ness, or the act is void. Does the master solemnly
covenant with his slave to emancipate him ? the
contract can be revoked at the master's will. No
extraordinary service of the slave, except in
North Carolina, would be held "a good consideration" and sufficient to bind the bargain. In
some States, as Maryland, and Virginia, in fact — no
person under thirty nor over five-and-forty can be
emancipated.

Take all the slave-laws of the United States
together, consider the Race that has made them,
their Religion, the Political Ideas of their government, that it is in the nineteenth century after Christ,
and they form the most revolting work of legislation to be found in the annals of any pacific people.
The codes of the Barbarians who sat on the ruins
of the Roman Empire — the Burgundians, Bava-
rians, the Allemanni, with the Visigoths and their
northern kin — have left enactments certainly

more terrible in themselves. But the darkness of
that period shrouds all those barbarian legislations
in a general and homogeneous gloom; and here, it
is " the freest and most enlightened nation of the
world," who keeps, extends, and intensifies the
dreadful statutes which make men only things,
binds and sells them as brute cattle. In 1102, the
Council of London decreed that " hereafter no one
shall presume to carry on the nefarious business in
which hitherto, men in England are wont to be
sold as brute beasts." The churches of America
have no voice of rebuke — no word of entreaty
when Christian Clergymen sell their brothers in
the market. The flag of America and the majesty
of the law defend that " business," which the
Anglo Saxon Bishops, seven hundred and forty-five
years ago, looked on as " nefarious," *Nefarium Ne-
gotium*. M. de Tocqueville regarded the American
slave-code as " Legislation stained by unparalleled
atrocities ; a despotism directed against the human
mind ; Legislation which forbids the slaves to be
taught to read and write, and which aims to sink
them as nearly as possible to the level of the
brutes."

The effect of Slavery appears in the general
legislation of the South. In Wisdom and Humanity it is far behind the North. It is there that laws
are most bloody ; punishments most barbarous and

vindictive ; that irregular violence takes most often
the place of legal procedure; that equity is least
sure even for the free whites themselves. One
end of the slave's chain is round the master's neck.
" Justice," says a proverb, " has feet of wool
but iron hands." The slave-driver's whip, and the
bowie-knife of the American have a near relation.

Some of the Southern States have enacted remarkable laws to this effect : That when any free
negro or person of color arrives in any vessel at a
Southern port, he shall be shut up in prison until
the departure of the vessel, the owner of the vessel
paying the costs. By this law the free citizens of
the free States are continually imprisoned in South
Carolina and Louisiana. This is not only a violation of the constitution of the United States, but
it is contrary to the common customs of Christian
nations ; a law without a parallel in their codes ; a
result which Gouverneur Morris did not anticipate
in 1787, when he made his satirical calculation
of the value of the Union to the North.

The iniquity of the code of the Slave States has
passed into some enactments of the general government of the Union. In 1793, a law was made by
Congress to this effect : A fugitive slave escaping
into a free State — and consequently *any man claimed to be such* — may be seized by the master or his

agent, and carried back to Slavery without the
intervention of a Trial by Jury to determine whether
the man is a slave — simply by a trial before
" any Judge of .the circuit or district courts of the
United States residing or being within the State,
or before any magistrate of the county, city, or
town corporate where such seizure or arrest shall
be made." The proof required that the man is a
slave is by " oral testimony or affidavit " of the
parties interested in the man's capture. This is a
departure from the Customs of your Fathers ; — a
departure which the Common Law of England
would not justify at any time since the Norman conquest. The Trial by Jury has been regarded the
great Safeguard of personal Freedom ; even in the
dark ages of English law it was the Right of every
man, of every fugitive slave, when his person was
in peril. Had a slave escaped, with his children,
and remained some time a freeman — *statu liber ;*
did the master find the children and not the father,
he could not hold them till he caught the father, and
by a jury-trial proved his claim. In the United
States the laws do not favor liberty in case of men
born with African blood in their veins.

The power of the general government has been
continually exercised against this class of Americans. It pursues them after they have taken refuge
with the Indians ; it has sullied the American name
by vainly asking the monarch of England to deliver

up fugitive American slaves who had fled to Canada and sought freedom under her flag.

The federal government established Slavery in the District of Columbia, in various Territories, and approved the constitutions of EIGHT new States which aim to perpetuate the institution.

For a long time the House of Representatives refused to receive " all petitions, memorials, resolutions and propositions relating in any way or to any extent whatever to the subject of Slavery." Thus have the " unalienable rights " of man been trampled under foot by the government of the most powerful Republic in the world. But last summer, in the city of Washington two women were sold as slaves, on account of the United States of America, by her marshal, at public auction !

But let us look at the POLITICAL EFFECT of Slavery. The existence of 3,000,000 slaves in the heart of the nation, with interests hostile to their masters weakens the effective force of the nation in time of war. It was found to be so in the Revolution, and in the late war. The slave States offer a most vulnerable point of attack. Let an enemy offer freedom to all the slaves who would join the standard — they will find " in every negro a decided friend," and the South could not stand with millions of foes scattered through all parts of her

territory. Have the slaves no arms ? There are
FIREBRANDS on every hearth. During the Revolution many thousands escaped from South Carolina
alone. At the conclusion of the last war with
England she offered to pay $1,204,000 as the
value of the slaves who, in a brief period, had taken
shelter beneath her flag. What if England had
armed them as soldiers — to ravage the country
and burn the towns ? Will a future enemy be so
reluctant ? The feeling of the civilized world re-
volts at our inhumanity. The English, for reasons
no longer existing, took little pains to avail themselves of the weapon thus thrust into their hands.
In the time of our troubles with France, when war
was expected, General Washington had serious
apprehensions from this source. Even in 1756,
during the French war, Governor Dinwiddie of
Virginia did not " dare venture to part with any of
our white men any distance, as we must have a
watchful eye over our negro slaves."

The Revolutionary war showed the respective
military abilities of North and South, and their respective devotion to their country's cause. It is
not easy, perhaps not possible to ascertain the sums
of money furnished by the particular States, for the
purposes of that war ; the number of men it is easy
to learn. Taking the census of 1790 as the standard, the six slave States had a free population of

1,852,504, or, including Kentucky and Tennessee, 1,961,372. Let us suppose, that during the Revolution, from 1775 to 1783, the number was but two thirds as great, or 1,307,549. In those States there were 657,527 slaves, all the other States had likewise slaves; but in New England there were but 3,886, their influence quite inconsiderable in military affairs. Let us therefore compare the number of men furnished for the war by New England and the six slave States. In 1790 the population of New England was 1,009,823. But let us suppose, as before, that from 1775 to 1783, it was, on an average, but two thirds as large, or 673,215. During the nine years of the Revolutionary war, New England furnished for the continental army 119,305 men; while the slave States, with a free population of 1,307,549, furnished but 59,336 men for the continental army. Besides that, the slave States furnished 10,123 militia men, and New England 29,324.

Let us compare a slave State, and a free one, of about equal population. In 1790, South Carolina contained 249,073 persons; Connecticut 238,141. Supposing the population, during the war, only two thirds as great as in 1790, then South Carolina contained 166,018, and Connecticut 158,760 persons. During the nine years of the war, South Carolina sent 6,417 soldiers to the continental army, and Connecticut 32,039. In 1790, Massachusetts con-

tained 475,257 souls ; during the Revolution, according to the above ratio, 316,838. While the
six slave States, with their free population of
1,307,549, furnished but 59,336 soldiers for the
continental army, and 10,123 militia men, Massachusetts alone sent 68,007 soldiers to the continental army and 15,155 militia. THUS shoulder to
shoulder Massachusetts and South Carolina went
through the Revolution, and felt the great arm of
Washington lean on them both for support.

By the Constitution of the United States, in the
apportionment of representatives to Congress, five
slaves count the same as three freemen. This is a
provision unknown in former national codes, rest-
ing on a principle un-democratic, detrimental to liberty, and hitherto unheard of: the principle of
allowing parts of a nation political power in proportion to the number of men which they hold in
bondage. It would have astonished the Heathen
Democracy of Athens long centuries ago. By this
arrangement, from 1789 to 1792, the South gained
seven representatives in the first Congress ; from
1795 to 1813 — fourteen ; from 1813 to 1823 —
nineteen ; from 1823 to 1833 — twenty-two ; from
1833 to 1843 — twenty-five. By the last apportionment bill, one representative is allowed for
70,680 free men, or a proportionate number of
slaves. By this arrangement, in a House of only

225 members, the South gains twenty representatives on account of her slaves — more than one twelfth part of the whole.

At present the North has 138 representatives for 9,728,922 souls ; or 9,727,893 free men ; one representative for each 70,492 free men. The South has 87 representatives. There are within the slave States 4,848,105 free men ; they have one representative for each 55,725 free persons.

In the next Presidential election the North will have 166 electoral votes ; the South 117. The North has an electoral vote for each 52,576 free men ; the South one for each 41,436. Part of this difference is due to the fact that in the South there are several small States. But twenty electoral votes are given by the South, on account of her property in slaves. But if slaves are merely property, there is no reason why Southern Negroes should be represented in Congress more than the Spindles of the North.

But the South pays direct taxes for her slaves in the same proportion. A direct tax has been resorted to only four times since 1789 by the General Government, viz. in 1798, 1813, 1814, and 1816. The whole amount assessed is $14,000,000. Of this about $12,750,000 was actually paid into the treasury of the United States, though part in a depreciated currency. Of that the South paid for

9*

her slaves, if the computation be correct, only $1,256,553.

In 1837 the surplus revenue of the Union, amounting to $37,468,859 97, was distributed among the several States in proportion to their electoral votes. By the census of 1830, the North had 7,008,451 free persons, and the South but 3,823,289. The free States received $21,410,777 12, and the slave States $16,058,082 85. Each free man of the North received but $3 05, while each free man of the South received $4 20 in that division.

At that time the South had one hundred and twenty-six electoral votes, of which twenty-five were on account of her slave-representation. She therefore received by that arrangement $3,186,127 50 on account of the representation of her slaves. From that if we deduct the $1,256,553 paid by her as direct taxes on her slaves, there is left $1,929,574 50, as the bonus which the South has received from the treasury of the Nation on account of the representation of slaves — Southern property represented in Congress. To this we must add $57,556, which the South received in 1842 from the sale of public land on account of her slaves, the sum is $1,987,130 50. Mr. Pinckney was right when he said the terms were not bad for the South.

Slavery diverts the freeman from Industry, from Science, from Letters and the Elegant Arts. It has been said to qualify him for Politics. As political matters have been managed in the United States in this century, the remark seems justified by the facts. Elections are not accidents. Of the eight Presidents elected in the nineteenth century, six were born in the South — children of the slave States. No northern man has ever twice been elected to the highest office of the Nation. A similar result appears in the appointment of important officers by the President himself. From 1789 to 1845, one hundred and seventy appointments were made of ministers and chargés to foreign powers; of these, seventy-eight were filled from the North, ninety-two from the South. Of the seventy-four ministers plenipotentiary sent to Europe before 1846, forty-three were from the slave States. There have been fifteen judges of the Supreme Court from the North; eighteen from the South. The office of Attorney General has been four times filled by Northern men, fourteen times by men from the slave States. Out of thirty Congresses, eleven only have had a Speaker from the North. These are significant facts, and plainly show the aptitude of Southern men to manage the political affairs of America. There are Pilots for fair weather; Pilots also only trusted in a Storm.

VII.

I AM now to speak of Slavery considered as a Wrong, an Offence against the natural and eternal Laws of God. You all know it is Wrong — a Crime against Humanity, a Sin before Almighty God. The great men who call Slavery — right and just ; — do they not know better ? The little and humble men who listen to their speech — do not we all know better ? Yes, we all know that Slavery is a Sin before God ; — is the union of many sins. On this theme I will say but a word.

The Roman code declares liberty the natural estate of man, but calls Slavery an institution of positive Law, by which one man is made subject to another, contrary to nature. By the Hebrew Law it was a capital offence to steal a man and sell him, or hold him as a Slave.

Now if that doctrine be true which the American people once solemnly declared self-evident — that all men are created with equal Rights — then every slave in the United States is stolen. Then Slavery is a continual and aggravated theft. It matters not that the slave's mother was stolen before. To take the child of a slave must be theft as much as to take the child of a freeman ; it is stealing mankind. He that murders a child has no defence in the fact that he first murdered the sire.

When we hear that the Emperor of Russia or Austria, for some political opinion, shuts a man in' the Spielberg, or sends him to Siberia, for life — we pity the victim of such despotic power, thinking his natural rights debarred. But the defence is that the man had shown himself dangerous to the welfare of the State, and so had justly forfeited his rights. When we reduce a man to a slave, making him a Thing — we can plead no extenuation of the offence. The slave is only " guilty of a skin not colored like our own," — guilty of the misfortune to be weak and unprotected. For this he is deprived of his liberty ; he and his children.

Slavery is against nature. It has no foundation in the permanent nature of man, in the nature of things, none in the eternal Law of God, as Reason and Conscience declare that Law. Its foundation is the selfishness, the tyranny of strong men. We all know it is so — the little and the great. Better say it at once, and with Mr. Rutledge declare that Religion and Humanity have nothing to do with the matter, than make the miserable pretence that it is consistent with Reason and accordant with Christianity; even the Boys know better.

In the last century your fathers cried out to God against the oppressions laid on them by England, justly cried out. Yet those oppressions were but little things — a tax on sugar, parchment, paper, tea; nothing but a tax, allowing no voice in the granting thereof or its spending. They went to war for an abstraction — the great doctrine of Human Rights. They declared themselves free, free by right of birth, free because born Men and children of God. For the justice of their cause they made solemn appeal to God Most High. What was the oppression the fathers suffered, to this their sons commit? It is no longer a question about Taxes and Representatives, a duty on sugar, parchment, paper, tea, but the liberty, the persons, the lives of three millions of Men are in question. You have taken their liberty, their persons, and render their lives bitter by oppression. Was it right in your fathers to draw the sword and slay the oppressor, who taxed them for his own purpose, taking but their money, nor much of that? Were your fathers noble men for their resistance? when they fell in battle did they fall "in the sacred cause of God and their country?" Do you build monuments to their memory and write thereon, "Sacred to Liberty and the Rights of Mankind"? Do you speak of Lexington and Bunker-Hill as spots most dear in the

soil of the New World, the Zion of Freedom, the
Thermopylæ of universal Right ?   Do you honor
the name of Washington far beyond all political
names of Conqueror or King ?   How then can you
justify your oppression ? how refuse to admit that the
bondmen of the United States have the same right,
and a far stronger inducement to draw the sword
and smite at your very life ?   Surely you cannot do
so, not in America ; never till Lexington and
Bunker-Hill are wiped out of the earth ; never till
the history of your own Revolution is forgot ; never
till the names of the Adamses, of Jefferson, of
Washington, is expunged from the memory of men.

When the rude African who rules over Dahomey
or the Gaboon country burns a village and plunders
the shrieking children of his fellow barbarians to
sell them away into bondage forever, far from
their humble but happy homes and their luxuriant
soil, their bread-fruit and their palms, far from
father and mother, from child and lover, from all
the human heart clings to with tenderest longing —
you are filled with horror at the deed.   " What !
steal a man," say you ; " Great God," you ask, " is
the Gaboon chieftain a man, or but a taller beast,
with mind more cunning and far reaching claws ? "
That chieftain is a barbarian.   He knows not your
letters, your laws, the tenets of your religion.   The
nobler nature of the man sleeps in his savage

breast.   His only plea is — his degradation.   His
defence before the world and before God is this:
He is a savage, he knows no law but force, no
right but only MIGHT alone.   For that plea and
defence the civilized man must excuse him, perhaps God holds him guiltless.

But when a civilized nation comes, with all the
art and science which mankind has learned in the
whole lifetime of the race, and steals the children
of the defenceless, stimulating the savage to plun-
der his brothers and make them slaves, the offence
has no such excuse ; it is a conscious crime; a
Wrong before the judgment of the nations; a Sin
before God.

In your case it is worse still ; the Autocrat of all
the Russias may have no theory of man's unalienable rights adverse to the Slavery he aims to abolish
on his broad estates and wide-spread realm; the
Bey of Tunis deals not in abstractions, in universal
laws, knows nothing of unalienable rights and the
inborn equality of man.   But you, the people of the
United States ; you, a nation of free men, who
owe allegiance to none ; you, a Republic, one of
the foremost nations of the Earth ; you with your
theories of human, universal justice; you who earliest
made national proclamation to mankind of human
right, and those three political ideas whereon the
great American commonwealth now stands and
rests ; you who profess to form a government not

on force, but law, not on national traditions, but
abstract justice — the Nation's constant and perpetual Will to give to every one his constant and perpetual Right ; you who would found a State not on
cannon balls — but Universal Laws, Thoughts of
God,— what plea can you put forth in your defence ?

You call yourselves Christians.   It is your boast.
"Christianity," say the courts, " is the Common Law
of the land."   You have a Religion which tells that
God is the Father, equal, just and loving, to all
mankind, — the Red man, whom you murdered,
and the Black man, whom you have laid in iron,
hurting his feet with fetters.   It tells you, all are
brothers, African, American, Red-man, and Black
and White.   It tells you, as your highest duty, to
love God with all your Heart ; to love his Justice,
love his Mercy, love his Love : to love that brother
as yourself — the more he needs, to love him still
the more ; that without such love for men there is
no love for God.   The Sacred Books of the nation — read in all pulpits, sworn over in all courts
of Justice, borne even in your war-ships, and
sheltered by the battle-flag of your armies — the
sacred books of the nation, tell, that Jesus, the
highest, dearest revelation of God to men, who loved
them all, that He laid down his life for them, for
all ; and bade you follow him !   What is a natural
action in the Savage, a mere mistake in the des

10

pot of Turkey or of Russia, with you becomes a
conscious and fearful wrong.   For you to hold
your Brothers in bondage, to keep them from all
chance of culture, growth in mind, or heart, or
soul ; for you to breed them as swine, and beat
as oxen ; to treat them as mere THINGS, without
soul, or Rights, — why, what was a mistake in
political economy, a wrong before your ideas of
Government, becomes a Sin foul and heinous before your ideas of Man, and Christ, and God.

When you remember the intelligence of this age,
its accumulated stores of Knowledge, Science, Art,
and Wealth of Matter and of Mind, its Knowledge
of Justice and eternal Right ; when you consider
that in political Ideas you stand the first people
in the vanguard of mankind, now moving towards
new and peaceful conquests for the human race ;
when you reflect on the great doctrines of Universal Right set forth in so many forms amongst you
by the senator and the school-boy ; when you bring
home to your bosoms the Religion whose sacred
words are taught in that Bible, laid up in your
churches, reverently kept in your courts of justice,
carried under the folds of your flag over land and
sea — that Bible, by millions multiplied and spread
throughout the peopled world in every barbarous
and stammering tongue, — and then remember that
Slavery is here ; that three million men are now
by Christian Republican America held in bondage

worse than Egyptian, hopeless as hell, — you must
take this matter to heart, and confess that American Slavery is the greatest, foulest Wrong which
man ever did to man ; the most hideous and detested Sin a nation has ever committed before the
just, all-bounteous God — a Wrong and a Sin
wholly without excuse.

CONCLUSION.

FELLOW-CITIZENS OF AMERICA,

You see some of the effects of Slavery in your land. It costs you millions of dollars each year. If there had been no slaves in America for forty years, it is within bounds to say, your annual earnings would be three hundred million dollars more than now. It has cost you also millions of men. But for this curse, Virginia had been as populous as New York, as rich in wealth and intelligence; without this the free men of the South must have increased as rapidly as in the North, and at this day, perhaps five-and-twenty million men would rejoice at their welfare in the United States. Slavery retards Industry in all its forms; the Education of the people in all its forms, intellectual, moral and religious. It hinders the application of those great political Ideas of America; hinders the Development of mankind, the Organization of the Rights of Man in a worthy State, Society, or

Church. Such effects are the Divine Sentence against the Cause thereof.

It is not for me to point out the Remedy for the evil, and show how it can be applied; that is work for those men you dignify with place and power. I pretend not to give counsel here, only to tell the warning truth. Will you say, that in the free States also there is Oppression, Ignorance, and Want and Crime? 'Tis true. But an excuse, specious and popular, for its continuance, is this: that the evils of Slavery are so much worse, men will not meddle with the less till the greater is removed. Men are so wonted to this monstrous wrong, they cannot see the little wrongs with which modern society is full; evils, which are little only when compared to that. When this shame of the nation is wiped off, it will be easy, seeing more clearly, to redress the minor ills of Ignorance and Want and Crime. But there is one bright thing connected with this Wrong. I mean the Heroism which wars against it with pure hands; historic times have seen no chivalry so heroic.

Not long ago Europe and the whole Christian world rung with indignation at the outrage said to be offered, by the Russian government, to some Polish nuns who were torn from their home, driven from place to place, brutally beaten, and vexed with continual torments. Be the story false or true, the

10*

ears of men tingled at the tale.   But not one of the
nuns was SOLD.   Those wrongs committed against
a few defenceless women are doubled, trebled in
America, and here continually applied to thousands of American women.   This is no fiction; a
plain fact, and notorious; but whose ears tingle?
Is it worse to abuse a few white women in Russia,
than a nation of black women in America?   Is
that worse for a European than this for the democratic Republicans of America?   The truth must
be spoken; the voice of the Bondman's blood cries
out to God against us; His justice shall make
reply.   How can America ask mercy, who has
never shown it there?

Civilization extends everywhere: the Russian
and the Hottentot feel its influence.   Christian men
send the Bible to every island in the Pacific sea.
Plenty becomes general; famine but rare.   The
Arts advance, the useful, the beautiful, with rapid
steps.   Machines begin to dispense with human
drudgery.   Comfort gets distributed through their
influence, more widely than ancient benefactors
dared to dream.   What were luxuries to our
fathers, attainable only by the rich, now find their
way to the humble home.   War — the old Demon
which once possessed each strong nation, making
it deaf and blind, but yet exceeding fierce, so that
no feebler one could pass near and be safe — War

is losing his hold of the Human Race, the Devil getting cast out by the finger of God.　The Day of Peace begins to dawn upon mankind, wandering so long in darkness, and watching for that happy Star. Science, Letters, Religion, break down the barriers betwixt man and man, 'twixt class and class.　The obstacles which severed nations once now join them.　Trade mediates between land and land — the gold entering where steel could never force its way.　New powers are developed to hasten the humanizing work; they post o'er land and ocean without rest, or serve our bidding while they stand and wait.　The very lightning comes down, is caught, and made the errand-boy of the nations. Steamships are shooting across the ocean, weaving East and West in one united web.　The soldier yields to the merchant.　The man-child of the old world, young but strong, carries bread to his Father in the hour of need.　The ambassadors of Science, Letters and the Arts, come from the old world to reside near the court of the New, telling truth for the common welfare of all.　The Genius of America sends also its first fruits and a Scion of its own green tree, a token of future blessings, to the parent land.　These things help the great synthesis of the Human Race, the Reign of Peace on Earth, of Good-will amongst all men.

Everywhere in the old world the Poor, the Igno-rant and the Oppressed, get looked after as never

before.   The Hero of Force is falling behind the
times; the Hero of Thought, of Love, is felt to deserve
the homage of Mankind.   The Pope of Rome himself
essays the Reformation of Italy; the King of Den-
mark sets free the slaves in his dominions, East and
West; the Russian Emperor liberates his serfs
from the milder bondage of the Sclavonian race;
his brother monarch of Turkey will have no slave-
market in the Mahometan metropolis, no shambles
there for human flesh; the Bey of Tunis cannot
bear a slave; it grieves his Islamitish heart, swarthy
African though he be.

Yet amid all this continual advance, America,
the first of the foremost nations to proclaim Equality, and Human Rights inborn with all; the first
confessedly to form a State on Nature's Law —
America restores Barbarism; will still hold slaves.
More despotic than Russia, more barbarous than
the chieftain of Barbary, she establishes Ferocity
by federal law.   There is suffering enough amongst
the Weak and Poor in the cities of the free labo-
rious North.   England has her misery patent to
the eye, and Ireland her looped and windowed rag-
gedness, her lean and brutal want.   So it is everywhere; there is sadness amid all the splendors of
modern science and civilization, though far less
than ever before.   But amidst the ills of Christen-
dom, the saddest and most ghastly spectacle on
earth is American Slavery.   The misery of the old

world grows less and less; the Monster-vice of America, to make itself more awful yet, must drag your cannon to invade new lands.

I have addressed you as citizens, Members of the State. I cannot forget that you are men; are members of the great Brotherhood of Man, children of the one and blessed God, whose equal Love has only made to bless us all, who will not suffer Wrong to pass without its due. Think of the nation's deed, done continually and afresh. God shall hear the voice of your Brother's blood, long crying from the ground; His Justice asks you even now; AMERICA, WHERE IS THY BROTHER? This is the answer which America must give: " Lo, he is there in the Rice-swamps of the South, in her fields teeming with Cotton and the luxuriant Cane. He was weak and I seized him; naked and I bound him; ignorant, poor and savage, and I over-mastered him. I laid on his feebler shoulders my grievous yoke. I have chained him with my fet-ters; beat him with my whip. Other tyrants had dominion over him, but my finger was thicker than their loins. I have branded the mark of my power, with red-hot iron upon his human flesh. I am fed with his toil; fat, voluptuous on his sweat, and tears and blood. I stole the Father, stole also the Sons, and set them to toil; his Wife and Daughters are a pleasant spoil to me. Behold the children also of thy servant and his Handmaidens — sons swarthier than their sire. Askest Thou for the African? I found him a Barbarian. I have made him a Beast. Lo, there thou hast what is thine."

That Voice shall speak again: "America, why dost thou use him thus — thine equal, born with Rights the same as thine?"

America, may answer: "Lord, I knew not the negro had a Right to freedom. I rejoiced to eat the labors of the slave; my great men, North and South, they told me Slavery was no wrong; I knew no better, but believed their word, for they are great, O Lord, and excellent."

That same Voice may answer yet again, quoting the nation's earliest and most patriotic words: "'All men are created equal, and endowed by their Creator with unalienable Rights — the Right to Life, to Liberty, and the Pursuit of Happiness.' America, what further falsehood wilt thou speak"?

The Nation may reply again: "True Lord, all that is written in the nation's creed, writ by my greatest spirits in their greatest hour. But since then, why, holy men have come and told me in thy name that Slavery was good; was right; that Thou thyself didst once establish it on earth, and He who spoke thy words, spoke nought against this thing. I have believed these men, for they are holy men O Lord, and excellent."

Then may that Judge of all the Earth take down

the Gospel from the pulpit's desk, and read these few plain words : " Thou shalt love the Lord thy God with all thy heart; and thou shalt love thy neighbor as thyself. Whatsoever ye would that others should do to you, do also even so to them."

Further might He speak and say : " While the poor Mussulman, whom thou calls't Pagan and shuts't out from Heaven — sets free all men, how much more art thou thyself condemned ; yea, by the Bible which thou sendest to the outcasts of the world ? "

Across the Stage of Time the nations pass in the solemn pomp of their historical procession ; what kingly forms sweep by, leading the nations of the past, the present age ! Let them pass — their mingled good and ill. A great People now comes forth, the newest born of nations, the latest Hope of Mankind, the Heir of sixty centuries — the Bridegroom of the virgin West. First come those PILGRIMS, few and far between, who knelt on the sands of a wilderness, whose depth they knew not, nor yet its prophecy, who meekly trusting in their God, in want and war, but wanting not in Faith, laid with their prayers the deep foundations of the State and Church. Then follow more majestic men, bringing great Truths for all Mankind, seized from the heaven of thought, or caught, ground-lightning, rushing from the earth ; and on their ban-

ners have they writ these words : EQUALITY AND
INBORN RIGHTS. Then comes the ONE with ven-
erable face, who ruled alike the Senate and the
Camp, and at whose feet the attendant years spread
garlands, laurel-wreaths, calling him First in War,
and First in Peace, and First in his Country's Heart,
as it in his. Then follow men bearing the first
fruits of our toil, the wealth of sea and land, the
labors of the loom, the stores of commerce and the
arts. A happy People comes, some with shut Bibles
in their hands, some with the nation's Laws, some
uttering those mighty Truths which God has writ
on Man, and men have copied into golden words.
Then comes, to close this long historic pomp, — the
panorama of the world — the NEGRO SLAVE, bought,
branded, beat.

    I remain your fellow-citizen and friend,

THEODORE PARKER.

Boston, December 22, 1847.